Thank You Very Much:

Gratitude Strategies to Create a Workplace Culture that ROCKS!

Lisa Ryan, CSP

Grategy, LLC

Thank You Very Much

Gratitude Strategies to Create a Workplace Culture that ROCKS!

By Lisa Ryan
Published by Grategy Press, Cleveland, Ohio
© 2022 Grategy, LLC

All rights reserved.
No part of this book may be reproduced in any form or by any means without prior written permission of Lisa Ryan.

In other words, please play nice. Ask before you use, and then give proper attribution to the author. Thank you!

Grategy, LLC
3222 Perl Ct.
North Royalton, OH 44133
216-359-1134

lisa@grategy.com
www.LisaRyanSpeaks.com

This book is dedicated to...

Thank you, Scott Ryan, for being my biggest cheerleader! Through all the changes and challenges that the pandemic caused to my business, and to our lives, I know I can always count on you for your love and support.

Thank you to my family who made the past two years a lot more fun on our twice-weekly Zoom calls. I know you're all not on every time, but it's always a blast to see: Roslynd Smith, Debbie and Brad Hollers, Christine and Tim Whitaker, Scott and Trisha Roman, Teresa Smith, Patricia and Phil Savilonis, Jennifer and Pete Syrmis (and Sophia), Brittany and Charlie Clark (and Isla), Brock Mladineo, Jenny Alleyne, Beverly Harries, Diane and Charles Noel, and Michele Case.

Thank you to my Mastermind Partners: Debbie Peterson, Justin Patton, John Register, Ted Ma, Mj Callaway, Maureen Zappala, and Annie Meehan for the endless hours you listened to me talk about this book and the ideas you gave me to finally get it done!

Thank you to everyone who shared their stories with me and allowed me to use their examples of a workplace culture that ROCKS! My awesome contributors include Ray Brown, Manny DeSantis, Theo Etzel, Dale Evraets, Allison Giddens, Katie Guerdan, Will Healy, John Hrdlick, Teresa

Lindsey, Paul McEwan, Karen Norheim, Steve Pacilio, Linda Stalvey, Dana Syndergaard, Laura Timbrook, and Jesika Young.

I appreciate YOU!

Have fun,

Lisa

Other Books by Lisa Ryan

Manufacturing Engagement: 98 Proven Strategies to Attract and Retain Your Industry's Top Talent

To Have and to Hold: 101 Smart Strategies to Engage Employees

The Upside of Down Times: Discovering the Power of Gratitude

The Verbal Hug: 101 Awesome Ways to Express Appreciation

Express Gratitude, Experience Good: A Daily Gratitude Journal

Thank You Notes: Your 30-Days of Gratitude Workbook

52 Weeks of Gratitude: Transformation Through Appreciation

52 More Week of Gratitude: Thank Your Way to Happiness

From Afraid to Speak to Paid to Speak: How Overcoming Public Speaking Anxiety Boosts Your Confidence and Career

With Excellence: 10 Powerful Strategies on How to Get More Out of Life, Finance, and Business

Table of Contents

Thank you!..1

Gratitude Strategies to Create a Company Culture that Rocks: Introduction 3

Leadership's Role in Employee Engagement 13

Elevating Your Employees' Experience: Case Study: Cimtech ... 25

How Leaders Create Recognition and Celebration Strategies that Work... 31

Strategies to Design Your Employee Recognition Program..... 41

Engage Your Employees Through Ethics, Internships, and Flextime: Case Study: Win-Tech 51

Train Your Leaders Well to Increase Retention 55

No Employee Ever Quit Because of Too Much Training 65

How to Reboot Your Company Culture: Case Study: Karen Norheim, American Crane and Equipment Corporation 73

Keys to Onboarding Employees to Maximize Your ROI 77

The Exit Interview May be Too Late, Try a Stay Interview Instead 85

How to Express Gratitude in a Remote Workplace: Case Study: Paul McEwan, Rea & Associates........................... 93

Remote Working: How to Connect with Employees, No Matter Where They Are 97

Use Your Website and Social Media to Showcase Your Company Culture 107

Volunteerism: Case Study: Teresa Lindsey, Channel Products. . . 113

Engagement Strategies to Elevate Employee Wellness and Mental Health 119

The Role of Safety on Employee Engagement 129

Additional Resources: Nontraditional Places to Find Employees . . 135

About the Author 141

To Order Additional Copies of This Book: 143

Bibliography: 145

Thank you!

First, Thank YOU very much for picking up this book! If you're looking for strategies to create a workplace culture that ROCKS, you're in the right place.

Take a wild guess. How many hours do you think the average person spends during their lifetime at work? You may be surprised to know that employees spend a whopping 90,000 hours at work during their careers. You probably also realize that life is too short to work at a toxic, life-draining, soul-sucking place of employment. When your employees feel that way and decide to take their skills elsewhere, it can wreak havoc on your business.

Don't let that happen to you!

The good news is that employee engagement doesn't take as much time, money, or effort as you may believe. Employees want to feel that their personal values match those of their employer. Actively engaged employees are not only more pleasant to be around, but they are also more profitable and productive in their jobs.

This book will give you ideas that you can adapt and implement in your organization, no matter your business. You will also learn from other leaders who created cultures that ROCK and understand the steps they took to do it.

Each chapter contains action ideas broken down into three categories: Individuals, Management, and Organization. First, you will see what you can do personally to take care of yourself, your career, and your colleagues. Next, you'll discover what you can do as a leader to work directly with your team. Finally, you'll realize the steps your organization must take to change your company culture at its roots.

Consider your business to be like a prized garden. As the gardener, you'll recognize the importance of the seeds you plant at the beginning of the process, the nurturing it takes to grow the results you want, and the bountiful harvest you'll receive from your efforts.

And, like a garden, the cycle never ends. You will always be looking for ways to kick things up a notch. You'll gather ideas to be creative, connect with your employees, and, most of all, have fun doing it.

Every few chapters, you'll find case studies about organizations that went the extra mile to redefine, recreate, and reboot their company culture. At the end of the case studies, you'll have the opportunity to reflect on ways you can implement similar strategies in your organization.

I wish you all the best in your journey to a "workplace culture that ROCKS." I appreciate YOU!

Lisa Ryan, CSP

Gratitude Strategies to Create a Company Culture that Rocks: Introduction

"Gratitude turns what we have into enough, and more. It turns denial into acceptance, chaos into order, confusion into clarity...it makes sense of our past, brings peace for today, and creates a vision for tomorrow."
~Melody Beattie

In today's workplace, why are gratitude and the concept of saying "Thank you very much" so important? Because it changes every aspect of your life – and your business. This book will give the tips, ideas, and strategies to change the world, or at least your workplace, one "thank you" at a time.

To set the foundation of this book, let's go back to the beginning, so you'll understand how I discovered the transformative power of appreciation.

In 2009, I went on a firewalk. That is not a euphemism; it was a walk across a twelve-foot bed of red-hot embers. The funny part about this is the 2009 firewalk wasn't my first one. I did my first one in 1989. Understandably, the first one was powerful because it feels like you can take on the world when you walk on fire.

However, it was the second firewalk that changed everything. As my friends and I drove home from this four-day intensive workshop, we were excited and ready to implement everything we had learned. But we also knew that if we didn't act on what we learned, everything would go right back to where it was before, and we didn't want that to happen – again. So, we opened a Facebook thread, and every day we shared what we learned, experiences we had, and people we met. Finally, my friend Mike said, "Why don't we also share three things we're grateful for?"

We did that every day and held each other accountable. It was that daily gratitude practice that changed everything. I was in medical sales at the time, and customers that I hadn't talked to for months were calling me, "Hey, Lisa, can you come in and sell me some stuff?" (Yes! I'll be right there!) There were two large facilities that I had been calling on for almost five years that seemed to close effortlessly. I noticed differences in my husband, who was becoming more verbally appreciative. All these things were changing, but the only thing I had changed was this practice of gratitude.

That's when the research started. I attended programs, read books and articles, and interviewed people to see if gratitude was more than this feel-good emotion that I had always ascribed to it. Finally, I found out that there was much more to appreciation than I previously thought.

One of the first books I read was "Thanks," by Dr. Robert Emmons - a Ph.D. professor at the University of California at Davis. Dr. Emmons took a group of students and divided them into three. He had the first group write down what they were grateful for, while the second group recorded all the troubles, hassles, and things that aggravated them. The third group simply recorded the day's events; they were the control group.

After ten weeks, he discovered that the gratitude group was 25% happier. Dr. Emmons attributed this percentage increase to the baseline in which the participants started the project. For ten weeks before the experiment, participants kept a journal in which they logged their feelings, relationships, aches, pains, etc. Dr. Emmons used that information to differentiate the chronically happy people from the chronically crabby people. Thus, he was able to determine the 25% increase.

In addition to the increase in happiness, the gratitude group exercised, on average, an hour and a half more per week than the other two groups. They had fewer physical ailments. They were more optimistic, joyful, and enthusiastic. When Dr. Emmons interviewed the gratitude group associates to see if they noticed any difference, he found that they did. They revealed that the gratitude group was more emotionally available and nicer to be around.

When you discover your gratitude strategy (or Grategy), it changes every aspect of your life. Before we get to the value of appreciation in the workplace, we're going to start with YOU. Once you experience the power of finding the good in your life, it's much easier to take that concept to the workplace.

So, how does gratitude change your perspective? Research shows that a regular gratitude practice rewires your brain. The key is consistency. However, forgive yourself and start again if you get out of the habit. Start and stop as many times as you need to establish a daily gratitude routine.

My three favorite practices are the gratitude journal, wins journal, and ABCs of gratitude.

Gratitude Journal: When you wake up in the morning, take a notebook or journal and write down five sentences starting with, "I am grateful for...." Add some detail so you can feel the emotion of the moment. People ask me all the time, "Do I really need to write this down? After all, I'm grateful all the time." The short answer is YES! When you write things down, you're feeling the pen in your hand. You're hearing the words and feeling the emotion of gratitude.

Another fantastic thing about writing your appreciation down is that when you have a terrible start to your day, you can turn back a couple of pages and remind yourself of the good things that you have in your life.

Although taking pen to paper is my practice of choice, there are plenty of online and app options to develop your own journaling practice. Many people find an app more convenient and accessible, making it a personal choice. Just make sure you choose the version that makes it most likely to use and establish the gratitude journaling habit. Also, don't be afraid to experiment with both formats and switch back and forth until you find the one that works best for your lifestyle, which may change over time.

Many people will tell me, "Well, I used to have a gratitude journal, but I got away from it." That's why I prefer a gratitude journal without dates in it. There's no guilt that way. When you have a journal with dates in it, you may miss a couple of days and feel that you must go back and fill it in or give up on it. When you don't have dates, then there's no guilt. The nice thing about journaling in the morning is that you can be grateful in advance. For example, you can write, "I'm so grateful that I had a productive meeting with my boss today," setting the expectation of a good outcome.

Wins journal: This practice involves writing down five good things that happened during the day before you turn out the lights and go to bed. After a particularly horrific day, this may be the more difficult practice to do, but again, it makes you realize that when you look for the good, you can always find it.

ABCs of gratitude: Each night when you go to bed, take a random letter in the alphabet and think of something that you're grateful for that begins with that letter. Then, continue in alphabetical order until you fall asleep. Now, there are nights when you will go through the alphabet, sometimes even twice. But in most instances, it'll only take five or six letters before you fall asleep.

Research proves that people who have a regular gratitude practice are awake less time before falling asleep. As a result, they sleep more soundly and awaken more refreshed. So, what's the moral of that story? Count your blessings, not sheep.

To get started, I invite you to take my 30-Day Gratitude Challenge that I call "Take Five and Thrive." For this practice, challenge yourself to find daily appreciation using one or all these practices:

1. Gratitude journal. As discussed above, write down five things you are grateful for each day.
2. Express appreciation to people verbally. As a bonus, look for people who aren't thanked very often and make it a point to acknowledge them.
3. Send a letter of appreciation. The letter of appreciation is to say thank you BECAUSE that person makes a difference in your life. "I

want to let you know how important you are to me. I just want to let you know how much I appreciate having you in my life."
4. Write a thank-you note. A thank you note is written to thank a person FOR something. "Thank you for the gift. Thank you for your time. Thank you for dinner."
5. Meditate on gratitude for at least five minutes.

Remember, when you tell someone that you appreciate them, you create a beautiful memory. But when you write it down, you create a treasure. In writing a letter of appreciation, Dr. Emmons' research shows that the person writing the letter gets just as much or more benefit than the recipient gains from receiving it. Both parties benefit.

I have conducted several "official" 30-day gratitude challenges. The funniest thing about the challenge is that at the end of the challenge, people would tell me, "I really enjoyed the 30-day challenge, and I'm so sorry that it's over." The challenge is to get you started in developing your habit, and it's terrific if you decide to keep up the practice. I've had my practice since 2009, and I can vouch for the fact that it's changed my life on every level.

To get the biggest bang for your buck, invite a friend, colleague, or family member to participate in the challenge with you. Not only will you help the other person tremendously, but you will also strengthen your relationship with them.

Not only does gratitude make you feel good, but it's also good for you. The Institute of HeartMath in California studies emotions and their impact on our physical wellbeing. They conducted one research study comparing frustration and appreciation and their effect on the heart. They took a group of people, hooked them up to monitors, put them through a period of frustration, and then evaluated how their heart beat afterward. Imagine what a lie detector test looks like – that's how your heart is beating when you are frustrated. Then they took that same group of people, hooked them up to monitors, and put them through a session of appreciation, gratitude, love, compassion. Their heartbeat was smooth and looked like it was in flow. What is that telling you? All those people you are letting live rent-free inside your head are killing you!

A second HeartMath study compared the impacts of anger and compassion on the immune system. They discovered that for every five minutes you spend in anger, you reduce the effectiveness of your immune system for six HOURS. Those same five minutes spent in compassion, however, elevate the performance of your immune system for those same six hours. As you rewire your brain for gratitude, you look at things differently. When you choose positive emotions, it directly impacts your health.

The next area impacted by appreciation is your relationship with others. You've probably heard the saying, "If you can't say anything nice, don't say anything at all." The Lisa Ryan addendum says, "But if you can say something nice, do." Many times, you may assume that people know how you feel about them. Instead, make a point to let them know. Perhaps you'll tell them, call them, text them, or write them a note. Give people tangible evidence of your appreciation of them.

To discover how the people in your life want to be appreciated, I recommend the book "The Five Love Languages" by Gary Chapman. You may also want to check out Paul White's version of the same thing called "The Five Languages of Appreciation in the Workplace." The Cliff Notes version of both books is we are wired to get our "love tank" filled in five different ways. They are affirmation, physical touch, acts of service, quality time, and gifts.

At the beginning of a relationship, we're all over it. We're sharing words of affirmation, physically touching, spending quality time, doing acts of service, and giving gifts. Unfortunately, over time, we revert to our primary love language, which may cause a disconnect with the other person if that is not their preferred way. It's essential to pay attention to the Platinum Rule, which states, "Do unto others as THEY would have done unto them." Notice the slight change from the Golden Rule – "Do unto others as you would have done unto you." That's the point.

Even when experiencing a challenging situation, like a worldwide pandemic, you can always find the good. One of my most significant gifts of Covid happened in April of 2020 when I told my mother we should get together as a family on Zoom. She replied, "I don't know anything about that technology stuff. I'm not going to do that." So instead of letting her off the hook and getting on FaceTime as we had always done, I said, "Nope, we're going to do a Zoom call."

The first session consisted of me, my mom, and my stepsister. After that, my sister and brother joined in. After that, our calls grew to include international family members as well. We've been doing Zoom calls twice a week, on Wednesday nights and Saturday afternoons ever since. Our largest group call had nineteen people representing Ohio, Massachusetts, Florida, Georgia, Nevada, California, Texas, England, Barbados, Trinidad, and Canada. We had time zones from England (five hours ahead) to California (three hours behind), but we still managed to get good participation in the call.

My niece, Brittany, and my cousin, Jen, announced their pregnancies on Zoom during our time together. We went through the entire process with them – complete with baby showers and meeting the little ones for the first time within days of their births. We've had surprise birthday parties, holiday meals, and many conversations that would have never happened had it not been for Covid. For this, I am very grateful.

Now that we've talked about the power of gratitude in terms of its personal benefits, the rest of this book will focus on bringing ideas, tips, and gratitude strategies (Grategies) into the workplace. Each chapter will conclude with three sets of action steps:

- What you can do as an **Individual**.
- What you can do as a member of **Management**.
- What the **Organization** can do to change the culture.

Gratitude Strategy Action ideas:

Individuals:

1. Choose a gratitude practice for yourself and stick with it for at least thirty days.
2. Invite a friend, colleague, or family member to join you in your practice.
3. Make a point to let the people in your life know how much you value and appreciate them.
4. Discover your "love language" as well as the love languages of those around you.

Management:

1. Make a point to thank your employees for the work they do. Be specific in your reason for thanking them, so they know what they are doing well.

2. Don't just focus on when things are going extraordinarily well. Pay attention when everything is running smoothly and call attention to that.
3. Start your meetings by allowing participants to share good news and to express their appreciation to others in the room.
4. Provide thank you notes, cards, bulletin boards, whiteboards, etc., for people to share their gratitude. For your remote team members, you may want to send letters "snail mail" as well as pick up the phone and incorporate gratitude into your virtual meetings.

Organization:

1. Conduct an employee survey to assess and set the baseline for your employees' engagement level.
2. Once you have the survey results, act as quickly as possible on fixing issues and giving feedback.
3. Give your managers the tools they need to recognize and acknowledge their team members regularly.

Leadership's Role in Employee Engagement

"Employees engage with employers and brands when they're treated as humans worthy of respect."
~Meghan M. Biro, Forbes

When I was in the welding industry, Dale Evraets was the best manager I've ever had. Dale was passionate about the industry while being incredibly supportive of his people. He joined me in my celebration when I was having a fantastic day. Dale was there to "talk me off the ledge" and get me back on track when things weren't going so well. He also listened to me, no matter how colorful my descriptions of my frustrations were.

I'm certainly not saying Dale was perfect. He had flaws as a leader. For example, when he wanted to add another sales rep in my territory, I begged him not to do that. I felt that my region was fully covered, and I didn't want to deal with some "rookie" in the field. When he went ahead and started interviewing for the newly created sales position, I put together my resume to see how marketable I was. Unfortunately for Dale, I discovered that I was pretty marketable with seventeen years of sales experience and an MBA. Ultimately, I left the company, and the industry, to pursue a career in health care.

Dale could never find someone to take my place, and he departed the company a few years later. However, the story does have a happy ending, in that Dale is still one of my closest friends. Being a good leader doesn't always mean that you agree with your subordinates, but it does suggest that you work through disagreements and maintain a positive working relationship.

It's true. People don't leave their job; they leave their managers. My territory discussion with Dale turned out to be THE conversation that inspired me to consider other job opportunities. Unfortunately, you as a leader have no idea when the conversation you have with one of your staff will be the one that makes them decide to take their skills elsewhere.

When it comes to a job, most people want work that matters, colleagues they like, and a manager they respect. Although employees may settle for a job and colleagues that are just okay, their manager can make or break that person's decision to stay.

Influential leaders devote their time to supporting their team and building trust, while ineffective managers waste time elevating their political capital and promoting their accomplishments. Not only do you as a leader want to build strong relationships with your staff, but you also want to pay attention to how your managers behave towards their team members. If you see any issues or conflicts, it's vital that you address those concerns, provide the necessary training, and adjust when necessary.

The quality of a company's management team has a significant impact on the culture's quality. Successful leaders constantly look for new methods to bring out the best in their employees. Dale, for example, recognized things in me that I didn't notice. His words of support gave me the courage to accomplish what I needed to do to achieve success. Leaders create possibilities for growth and development based on an employee's individual skills rather than a pre-determined, one-size-fits-all career path.

Linda Stalvey works with Cutler Real Estate. Her leadership team encourages its agents to follow a morning routine of giving thanks for what they have, for those around them, and for who they are. Company leaders advise their team to start their day by reading something positive and focusing on a goal as if they've already achieved it. Agents write positive affirmations to help them achieve their goals, and they show appreciation to each other by writing personal notes.

Why do their leaders prioritize positivity? They want their agents to get into the habit of programming themselves every day to be vibrating and sending/receiving energy frequencies of gratitude, love, abundance, and positive expectation.

Aside from emphasizing personal growth and development, Cutler's broker-owner and the leadership team argue that their agents don't work for the company – the leadership works for their team members. Building relationships is key to realtor success at Cutler. The company provides the technology at no (or low) cost to allow their agent to provide pertinent information—not sales pitches—to their clientele and sphere.

Every agent is celebrated – from the ones who sell $50 million a year to the one who sells their first house at $60,000. All employees check their egos at the door. If a person's ego is oversized, they are not a fit to work there.

As shown in the Cutler example, employees want leaders they can trust and who empower them to be the best versions of themselves. In the workplace, as in life, loyalty is hard to earn and easy to lose. There are no shortcuts. Commitment is yours only when you deserve it. When your employees don't feel recognized and valued for their excellent work, there is little infrastructure to foster trust and loyalty. Leaders instill a commitment in their teams by connecting them with a vision, mission, and core cultural values. This commitment builds a unique link between employees and "the boss."

It all comes down to creating the culture that encourages your employees to stay with your organization. Turnover is expensive, but you may not realize how much voluntary turnover costs you until you put pen to paper. So, the first step is to determine how much you are spending to bring employees in the door – recruiting, onboarding, training, etc. – and what it costs when they leave. Because you can't manage what you can't measure, you'll want to start by determining your retention rate's baseline. Having these figures in hand is a powerful motivator to make the required changes to boost your engagement levels, which will help you retain more customers.

Select the period for which you wish to calculate your turnover rates. Most organizations use quarterly or annual turnover rate statistics to highlight more relevant patterns. You may also want to isolate and separately measure new hire turnover rates because new hires leave for reasons that are not always the same as those of their tenured counterparts. When calculated, these numbers help employers pinpoint and resolve issues faster. Another best practice is to calculate voluntary turnovers separately, as these numbers may reflect your company's competitiveness compared to other employers.

Here are some formulas you can use to calculate the employee turnover rate in your organization:

Turnover calculation:

Start by calculating the average number of employees for the period. To do this, add: (# of employees at the beginning of the period) + (# of employees at the end of the period), and divide by two.

Divide: (# of employees who separated from the company during that period) by (average # of employees)

Multiply: (# calculated in step 2) x 100 = turnover percentage

First-year turnover rate

You will use only the number of separated employees who worked for less than a year in this computation. For a given year, replace the average number of employees with the actual number of separations.

Calculate the total number of employee separations – both voluntary and involuntary – within 12 months.

Divide: (# of separated employees who worked at the company less than one year) by (# of all separations)

Multiply: (# calculated in step 2) x 100 = turnover percentage

Now that you've figured out your turnover rate, it will be easier to observe the positive changes brought about by your retention initiatives. However, no matter where you are initially, keep in mind that employee engagement is not a "one and done" event. Impactful leaders continue to survey their team to uncover what's working and any improvements employees would like to see. The key is to commit to one or two priorities as determined by your staff and act on them. Include as many individuals as possible in your decision-making as you learn and adjust.

Employees are the foundation of any organization, and if that foundation begins to crack, your whole company can come tumbling down. But, on the other hand, when you have your employees' best interests at heart, and they know you care about them, they are more likely to trust you and perform at a higher standard.

According to research, employees who work for inclusive leaders are 39 percent more likely to be engaged. In addition, because employees come in many shapes, sizes, colors, and talents, you want to make sure your leadership team reflects the diversity of the workforce. Not only is this a good idea from a legal standpoint, but it's also critical to attracting the best and brightest talent coming into the workplace.

My husband spent more than thirteen years in his previous job. He became part of the "Great Resignation" when he reconsidered his professional path after his firm furloughed him because of the pandemic. Even though he had been miserable for several years, he had no desire to leave. He felt at ease in his position and knew what his boss expected from him. During his leave, he realized that his managers focused their feedback on what he was doing wrong. They seldom acknowledged him for excellent work and gave him no feedback when things were smoothly running. That expectation of "that's his job, and we don't have to thank him for it" took a toll on him, which became apparent in his furlough-based career reassessment.

Scott concluded that his current employer was not where he wanted to complete his career. However, even after being called back to work and returning to the status quo, he decided to keep his options open. After a few months back on the job, one of those choices came to fruition, and he accepted a new position.

Scott seized the opportunity, and I'm delighted to report that he is happy now. I regularly hear his stories, including the utter disbelief he felt when a salesperson came in and thanked him for his help on a project. On another occasion, when he manually completed an assignment when the computers were down, his boss, Katie, texted him and let him know that he did a good job, and she appreciated it. Seemingly insignificant details can create or destroy an employee's connection and degree of trust.

Contrary to common opinion, there is no such thing as a natural-born leader. Some people have stronger people skills than others when engaging their colleagues, but the intentional leader stands out. The dedication to acquiring and maintaining the abilities required to be the best leader possible is the definition of intentional leadership. Intentional leaders not only invest in their own personal and professional development, but they also provide development opportunities and resources for their employees. They encourage their team members to take advantage of these programs. In addition, these leaders reduce the risk of losing their upwardly mobile people by investing in their future and creating a clear succession plan.

What other characteristics set intentional leaders apart from their less effective counterparts? One of the most prominent attributes is that they appreciate their team members. They realize that what gets recognized gets results, so they look to catch their employees in the act of doing things well and acknowledge them for their efforts. Expressing gratitude for a job well done goes a long way in connecting with employees.

Your employees want to know when they are doing things well. A participant in one of my programs told me, "When I do something wrong, I get recognized 100% of the time. When I do something well, my managers rarely notice." It's the little things that count. Thank your employees regularly. It makes a difference.

Marcial Francisco Losada (1939–2020), a Chilean psychologist, consultant, and former director of the Center for Advanced Research (CFAR) in Ann Arbor, Michigan, studied high-performing teams' characteristics. He discovered that the highest performing teams worked on a 6:1 positivity ratio. In other words, for every one negative comment a team member would hear from a colleague or boss, they would listen to at least six positive remarks. Moreover, these positive remarks are not gratuitous; they are sincere and specific.

The positivity ratio drops to 3:1 — three positives for every negative on average-performing teams. When you have this ratio, your team is performing at a level that is considered neutral. To put it another way, they're working just enough to avoid being fired, and you're presumably paying them just enough to keep them from quitting.

However, on a low-performing team, the ratio collapses to .3:1 (point three to one). In other words, employees hear three times more negative comments than positive remarks. Many managers believe they are doing their job by fixing what's broken and getting their employees to "shape up or ship out." Unfortunately, it doesn't work. Your "problem children" are not inspired by your negative feedback, nor are they going to change because you want them to. Focusing on your team members' good work will encourage them to give their best to you and your company.

It's not only about expressing appreciation but communicating all areas of the business. Great managers ensure that employees know what's going on – the good, the bad, and the ugly. They share information at all levels of the organization and let employees feel that they are part of the big picture.

My health care career ended when management blindsided nineteen of us during a conference call when we found out they eliminated our positions – effective immediately. The surviving employees dreaded every phone contact, meeting, and corporate communication for several years since they didn't know if they'd end up in the same situation as us. We could have been more prepared and trusted that management was doing the best they could with their problem if leadership had reached out to the employees and informed us of what was going on.

Whether the news is good or bad, convey relevant information early and often and in various modes. Managers may think they are overcommunicating to their team members and have the "I told them once, why should I have to tell them again" mentality, but they realize that it works over time. Having an open-door policy is excellent for the people in the office, while regular check-ins via phone, email and Zoom help support your remote staff. Offer opportunities for impromptu calls as needed to allow all employees – onsite and remote – to voice their problems and feedback in the manner they like to communicate.

It's essential to listen to what your employees share with you without judgment. No matter what they tell you, make sure you have a "thank you for sharing" attitude. Look for grains of truth – no matter how difficult their words are for you to hear. Whenever possible, act on their ideas and give credit where it is due. When employees see you paying attention and rewarding quality, they are more likely to offer their thoughts and opinions. You make it possible for them to do so in a safe environment.

Taking the effort to actively listen to and understand your employees' needs and problems will build your working relationship. Allowing employees to express burnout or overwhelming emotions should be done with empathy. Ascertain that they have access to employee support programs and have the resources they require to maintain their mental and physical well-being. These actions demonstrate that you care about them both personally and professionally.

Trust means that you empower your employees to do their job the best way they see fit while managing the accountability process. When you treat employees like you trust them to do a great job, they usually do just that. This is because your employees are more knowledgeable about their jobs than you are. They may not do it exactly the way you would, but they will frequently surprise you with their creativity and intelligence if given a chance.

Leaders build loyalty and trust with their team members by recognizing employees authentically. For example, when you send your team members a personal email or a handwritten note to show that you are personally aware of and appreciate their hard work, they feel valued and appreciated by you. Likewise, you build loyalty and commitment to your organization when you celebrate birthdays and anniversaries to make the employee feel special on their big day.

To keep engagement levels high, you may at times have to make the painful decision to fire toxic employees. (Note: Make sure you have proper documentation of the employee's bad behavior, so you don't find yourself on the opposite end of a wrongful termination lawsuit.) Terminating people is never easy, especially in a market where employees are already hard to come by. Employees become demotivated when they witness their teammates get away with bad behavior and terrible attitudes, and they no longer want to offer their all. When employees know that you are willing to terminate employees who don't support the organization's core values, the remaining team members feel more loyal to the leadership team.

It took a long time for your organization to develop its culture. It isn't going to change in an instant. Employee engagement is a long-term strategy built on leadership and employee trust, integrity, two-way commitment, and communication. Remember that engagement begins at the top. If your executive team blames human resources or lower-level supervisors, it won't work. That's unfortunate, but it's the truth.

Engaged employees have a deep, emotional connection to your company. Not only are they your hardest workers, but they are also the ones who stay with you for the long term and make the most significant contributions to the bottom line.

Leadership and the Engaged Employee: Action Ideas:

Individuals:

1. Invest in your personal and professional development to ensure your skills are up to date. Listen to audiobooks and podcasts on topics of interest in your spare time. Check out YouTube videos to learn just about anything you want to know.
2. Thank and acknowledge your colleagues for the excellent work that they do. Be specific and let them know why they matter.
3. Make a list of your biggest strengths and what you like most about your job. Look for opportunities to build on your strengths and do more of what you love to do.

Management:

1. Put pen to paper and figure out your actual turnover statistics and associated costs. Use this number as a baseline to compare your new rates after adopting an engagement program.
2. Include as many employees in your engagement program plans as possible. Invite people from different departments and levels to collaborate on your initiatives.
3. Make a point to acknowledge the excellent work of your employees and catch them in the act of going things well. Give them tangible evidence of a job well done – a handwritten note means a lot to the recipient.
4. Listen to your employees' feedback without judgment and find any kernels of truth in their commentary. Although it may be difficult to hear, if an employee trusts you enough to share their thoughts, it's up to you to see how you can help.
5. Terminate employees who refuse to go along with your initiatives, no matter how good they are at their job (with proper documentation, of course). This example lets the rest of your staff know that you have their backs and will not tolerate bad behavior.

Organization:

1. Create a culture of transparency. Share all relevant company news and events that impact your employees and leadership team.
2. Corporate success is not only about making your numbers. Provide employee assistance programs and resources for employees going through tough times.
3. Do not tolerate bad behavior from your managers. For example, when you notice a manager with an unusually high turnover rate in their department, take steps to shape them up or ship them out.

Elevating Your Employees' Experience: Case Study: Cimtech

"There's no magic formula for great company culture. The key is just to treat your staff how you would like to be treated."
~ Richard Branson

What would it look like if you had the opportunity to build your culture from the ground up? Jesika Young purchased a manufacturing company, although she had no direct manufacturing experience whatsoever. Although she grew up in manufacturing and loved being around fabricators like her father, her career started in the banking industry. Ten years later, when she had had enough of the corporate world, she decided to pursue a new path and purchase, Cimtech, a 43-year-old manufacturing company.

As Jesika learned the business, she trained in assembly and on the fork trucks to learn from everyone she worked with. Jesika also realized that she needed to reassess the value she believed she brought to the company. With an average employee tenure of 20 years, Jesika knew her value wasn't in operating CNC machines or welding; it was in her ability to create a great workplace culture. She decided to focus on the employee experience and adopted the philosophy that no one is above anyone else. People were no longer "employees"; they became "teammates."

She implemented new systems for communication and collaboration and focused on sharing company goals and objectives, communicating their "why," and how they wanted to grow. Jesika's leadership team let their team members know that they were a vital part of the company, and they valued their ability to help the company grow.

One of the first changes they implemented was to change everyone's business card and their email signature title to "Team Member." Next, they revamped the employee handbook, striking out the word "employee." Jesika says, "If we onboard new team members, their business card and the paperwork says "team member" first and then machinist, welder, etc." They also changed their uniforms to Cimtech logo wear. Every team member has logo wear, and they're proud of it. They're wearing it as they go out and about, and it helps them feel that they're part of the team.

Another tradition that Jesika brought to her team is the "caught you being awesome" cards. Team members have access to stationery they can use whenever they want. When a team member goes above and beyond, a peer or a manager signs a card and explains what that person did that was awesome, and they thank them for being a great team member. The whole team signs the card, and it's a constant morale boost to feel appreciated - not just from an owner or a supervisor, but from your teammates.

Once a month, Cimtech holds team member lunches, where everyone breaks bread together. In addition, they share their favorite recipes and compete in grilling and meat smoking competitions.

From a manufacturing standpoint, a unique program they implemented is flexible scheduling. Jesika believes that "Life happens, things happen. You might oversleep. You might be a few minutes late." Therefore, each team member gets to choose their start time and (within some parameters) their lunch schedule. So, for example, if a team member has a doctor's appointment that will take two hours, they can take it during their lunch break and then make up that time on the backside.

The key to the success of their flexible scheduling program is communication. Jesika enjoys seeing her team members' excitement when they get to take their significant other out to lunch. She often hears the cheer, "Yay, flextime!" Or, if a team member occasionally wants to sleep in, they can also make up that later that day or that week.

At the beginning of the program, she had some members of management object to the concept of flexible scheduling. Managers shared comments like, "What if someone doesn't want to start at this time or wants to start earlier? How are we going to run production? Who's going to be here to run the equipment?" And so forth. Jesika suggested that they lay out everything that could possibly go wrong and then work backward to find solutions. After much discussion and rework, they rolled out the program to their team. Two years into the program, productivity has gone up, and her teammates love it. Best of all, it's been a great way to attract other people to Cimtech.

These are just a few ways that Jesika creates a team culture where everyone feels valued and included in the organization's success. When reflecting on building the team culture, the three factors that contribute to culture are abundantly clear. These factors are collaboration, communication, and consistency.

Here's how Jesika describes these factors.

Collaboration. To be engaged, employees must feel valued and included. Every team member brings a set of core strengths. Leaders need to focus on their employees' strengths. After all, every person brings their own unique background, thinking style, experiences, and operating rhythm. Every decision made should answer the question, what positive impact will it have on the team? Collaboration allows employees to flush ideas and avoid obstacles. The best ideas come from bringing team members together to accomplish the task.

Communication. It's vital to communicate the organization's WHY. Why are we doing this? Why does it matter? By articulating clearly the why, the team will become unified in the goal. It is essential to communicate the WHAT. What role will we each be playing the success? What should we avoid? What could we do differently? It's crucial to keep the ego out of it, remember communication is about the team.

Communicate the HOW. How are we going to accomplish our goals? By connecting and setting goals, the team culture will continue to flourish. Everyone deserves to be heard.

No matter how small, communicating wins creates momentum and excitement within the team. By sharing the losses, employees understand where things went wrong, which will bring the team even closer together. It becomes a learning experience. There is no such thing as over-communicating.

Consistency. Consistency is the hinge that brings it all together. Without consistent collaboration and communication, there is no team. By consistently thinking, "what impact will this have on the team?" you're inviting each team member to have a 'seat at the table' for collaboration and communicating the vision.

The power is in being consistent! Your culture should live and breathe Collaboration, Communication, and Consistency! Build a team culture where collaboration and communication are the expectation. It should become as natural as breathing. After all, it's the team, above all else.

Reflection Questions:

1. Are there opportunities for you to change the words you use to create a more positive workplace culture - such as changing "employees" to "team members" or "associates?"
2. In what ways can you catch your employees in the act of doing things well and acknowledge them for their efforts?
3. What can you do to add flexibility to your team members' schedules? Although there are many jobs that team members cannot do from a remote location, is it possible to create a more flexible schedule?
4. How can you better collaborate with your team members and take advantage of their strengths in your organization?
5. How can you be more transparent in your communication with your team?

How Leaders Create Recognition and Celebration Strategies that Work

> *"I have always believed that the way you treat your employees is the way you will treat your customers and that people flourish when they are praised."*
> ~ Richard Branson

In his forty-four-year career with INX International, John Hrdlick worked his way up from the production floor to President of the organization. He realized very early on that if he focused on his people, those employees would, in turn, take care of their customers. Therefore, nurturing their team members is the key to INX International's high retention rates.

One of the ways John celebrates his employees is to send out handwritten anniversary cards to team members who are celebrating milestone anniversaries. He writes approximately 12-15 notes every month to his people. John personalizes each card to add something that he knows about the recipient. Although he takes about two hours per month to complete the cards, he breaks up his writing sessions, so the notes don't all have to be written in one sitting. When his hand gets tired or his writing becomes illegible, he takes a break and picks up his pen again when he's ready. His staff truly appreciates the time and attention John devotes to making them feel valued in the company.

Along with his management team, John makes a point to walk the shop floor and talk to the staff. Managers find out what's working and what's not. They inquire about resources the team needs to do their job and their ideas to improve production efficiency. They get the employees directly involved, which increases their buy-in.

Employees see John and the various division vice presidents walking around and chatting with their colleagues, and leaders build one-on-one relationships because of these informal conversations. The employees' ideas and insights received also help make the company more efficient.

When employees work on team projects, they have the opportunity to present their ideas to leadership. Managers ask them questions and consider whether it's an idea they can act upon. If leaders reject the idea, the supervisor explains the denial. When project ideas are accepted, managers recognize the employees for a job well done. Whether the project represents slight or considerable savings, employees put their efforts into helping the company perform better, and the leadership team shows their appreciation for that.

John's leadership philosophy is a simple one, "It's not all about the numbers. Of course, the numbers are very important. But if you take care of your people, you take care of your customers, and you treat them as human beings, the result is the numbers will take care of themselves."

Although it's a bit of a cliché, it's true - people don't leave their job, they leave their managers. And in this era of the "Great Resignation," the relationship between supervisors and their team members can determine whether employees decide to stay.

Katie Guerdan, Manager of HR at TX Team, shares that every month, the COO sends out an email to all their leaders to obtain the names of folks who exhibit their "Values in Action." Each month, the company highlights a different value. When the leader provides the COO with that individual's name and an example of how they are exhibiting that value, the COO HAND WRITES thank you cards to them. It doesn't matter how many people are submitted; a handwritten card provides her recognition and gratitude.

Another thing that Katie's COO does to set herself apart, is that she personally calls each new hire before they start to welcome them to our team. Then, together with their CEO, handwrites anniversary and birthday cards sent to associates.

As in the case with John and Katie's leadership team, when it comes to their job, employees want work that matters, colleagues they like, and a manager they respect. Although employees may settle for a job and colleagues that are just okay, it's the manager that can make or break that person's decision to stay.

Here are five characteristics of great managers.

1. **They are appreciative**. What gets recognized gets results. Great managers look to catch their employees in the act of doing things well, and they acknowledge them for their efforts. They personalize the recognition by finding out their employees' favorite things: restaurant, candy bar, sports team, hobby, etc. Recognizing how THEY like to be acknowledged goes a long way in forming a connection with their employees.

2. **They are communicative**. Great managers ensure that employees know what's going on – the good, the bad, and the ugly. They provide information at all levels of the organization so employees feel part of the bigger picture. Because of the numerous ways available to communicate and different preferences in how people like to receive information, great managers reach out in various ways and focus on the mode their individual team members prefer.

3. **They are observant**. Great managers look for ways to bring out the best in their employees. They invest in their people and provide opportunities for growth and development based on their individual strengths - not on some cookie-cutter career plan. First, they help set career planning goals and ask their employees where they see themselves in one year, five years, and perhaps further. Then, they help their staff members reach their development goals by providing the necessary resources to achieve them.

4. **They encourage peer-to-peer recognition**. Great managers give employees opportunities to recognize and praise each other. For example, they may open staff meetings by allowing participants to share kudos and publicly thank team members. Not only does it feel good to be acknowledged by one's peers, but it also creates accountability among team members. Management's appreciation is one thing but feeling recognized by their colleagues makes individual performers feel integral to the team.

Peer-to-peer recognition also gives employees opportunities to create work relationships. These friendships are essential because Gallup's research finds that actively engaged employees have a "best friend" at work. Now, Gallup doesn't say "good friend," nor do they say, "people I tolerate," they say, "best friend." Why does that matter? Because it's a lot harder to leave a job where your best friend also happens to work.

What are some ways you can allow workplace friendships to occur? Here are three areas on which to focus:

1. **Socialize outside of the office.** When employees enjoy spending time with their coworkers, they are more likely to be excited about coming to work. Planning events outside of business hours is a great way to build bonds of friendship. Playing together also improves collaboration and trust between colleagues while at work.
2. **Participate in service projects.** Employees who volunteer together stay together. When leaders set aside time for their team to get involved in a charitable cause, lots of good things happen. Not only does volunteering offer health benefits to the participants (stress reduction, relationship building, and "helper's high"), but when potential candidates see a company that cares about the surrounding community, they're more likely to apply to join the organization.
3. **Celebrate each other.** When employees feel that their contributions are valued, they are more engaged and energized at work. The acknowledgment shouldn't only come from leaders – as mentioned above, make peer-to-peer recognition a part of your culture. When you give employees the time to recognize their peers for small achievements as they happen, you create higher levels of accountability and engagement.

Another excellent leadership example is Theo Etzel, Chairman of Conditioned Air. Theo recognizes his employees in several ways. One of the unique ways is through his open-book management style, where he shares the company's numbers with his employees.

Theo realized that they often lost employees because the workers were familiar with the approximate cost of the job they installed and then considered what the company was paying them to do it. In their calculations, they believed the company owners were "shoveling dollar bills into their pockets," and some of them decided they could go out and do the same thing on their own, keeping all that cash for themselves.

After reading *The Great Game of Business* by Jack Stack, Theo decided to implement the open-book management concept to see how it would work in their business. They started the process as an educational activity. Because most people weren't used to looking at a profit and loss statement, Theo made it into a guessing game.

He asked employees questions like, "How much do you think we spent on gas last month?", "What do you think it costs to get our vans to everybody's home?" "How much do you think we spend on insurance, training, tools, and everything else that goes into running the business?" The employees were astonished when they learned what the actual numbers were. Not only did they appreciate the fact that Theo trusted them enough to share the numbers, but several of them also decided that it wasn't worth the time or effort to go into business for themselves, and so they stayed.

After the employees were comfortable with the costs of doing business, Theo began to educate them on the income side. Their CFO would go through the line items, including health insurance, vacation time, and benefits - all the things that make up the expense side of the business. (No, they did not share salaries or personal information with employees). It was a very eye-opening experience for most employees. Theo feels that if you share this kind of information and ask your people to think about how to do things more efficiently to create greater value for the company, you need to share part of the profits that result from their efforts. Besides being the right thing to do, profit-sharing instills an owner's mentality in your team.

At the end of each year, they divide a portion of the profits and share it with employees. They found that it's a great way to involve people in the company's running, thank people for their excellent work, and encourage them to think about the bigger picture - again instilling an ownership mentality in all their team members. In addition to the workplace benefits, employees gained a better understanding of their personal finances, which helped to reduce their stress and increase their savings.

Theo looks at his employees holistically. He wants to make sure he knows about their families, what's going on in their lives, and if there are opportunities to assist them with challenging situations they may face. Theo believes when they support their team members on all fronts, they create a more unified team of people who like each other, work well together, and stay together. He believes that creating the right workplace atmosphere is essential to having a solid team. That includes recognizing people and catching them in the act of doing the right thing, telling employees they're doing an excellent job, patting them on the back, and making sure to do it publicly so that other employees see you congratulating their colleagues.

Theo's philosophy is that the most important thing that a leader can do is invest in their people. It's all about the team. Management must be willing to serve people, be transparent, be honest with them, and expect honesty from them. When you show respect and admiration for the people working for you, you gain their respect in return. Employees want to know you'll be with them when times are tough, and they trust you to openly admit when times are rough. In doing these things, you'll create the type of workplace culture that keeps your top talent and attracts more great people to your company.

Recognition and Celebration: Action Ideas:

Individuals:

1. Remember that every interaction you have during the day creates a "moment" with that individual. Always keep your interactions positive and respectful as you don't know what that other person may be going through.
2. Give your colleagues tangible evidence of your appreciation. Fist bumps are great, but a handwritten note can make that other person's day.
3. Celebrate the small wins in your life and the lives of your loved ones. Life is too short for good deeds to go unnoticed.

Management:

1. Catch your employees in the act of doing things well. Recognize and acknowledge their efforts in the way they like to be recognized. Instead of fixing what's broken, focus on excellent work and the times when everything is running smoothly.
2. Create "All About Me" sheets for your employees and find out their favorite things – a candy bar, hobby, sports team, restaurant, etc. Recognize them in the way that THEY want to be recognized by personalizing your acknowledgment. Also, give the recognition at the time something good happens.
3. Put together a list of ideas that you and your leadership team can use to recognize employees. Remember, it doesn't have to take a lot of time or money to do so. Your creative thought and attention to detail are what matter to your employees.

Organization:

1. Conduct an employee survey to determine how employees feel about working for you and what areas they'd like to see improvement. Act on their ideas and suggestions as quickly as possible and give credit where credit is due.
2. Consider opening your books and sharing company information with your team members. You'll not only build trust, but you may also receive ideas and suggestions to help you make or save money.
3. Make sure all your managers recognize their team members appropriately and consistently. The chances are good that you have some managers who are better and more comfortable in the process. Provide resources and training for managers who need to improve.

Strategies to Design Your Employee Recognition Program

> *"In behavioral economic terms, when we offer recognition, we are acknowledging that the recipients have met a social ideal. If we then recognize that behavior with praise or appreciation, we offer a confirmation that their behavior is desirable, and do so in a manner that recipients find meaningful."*
> ~Cindy Ventrice

Employees want to feel that they are part of something bigger than themselves. By allowing them to recognize and get to know each other, you create a more engaged culture.

Jesika Young, President of Cimtech, is constantly on the lookout for ways to make her team members feel valued and build her company's unique culture. She does that by recognizing and celebrating her team in many ways. Here are just a few creative ideas that she's using, and you can easily adapt them for your team.

- Fist bumps and handshakes
- Recognition cards
- Favorite candy, ice cream, donuts – food (just about) always works!

- Forklift certification
- Tailgate parties
- Ornament decoration parties
- Annual block party and barbeque
- Mother's Day/Father's Day cards
- Random acts of kindness days
- Trading in kudos cards for cash prizes
- Thanksgiving gift cards and meals for team members and needy families
- Gratitude signs posted throughout the plant

Jesika enjoys these celebrations and has seen how much higher productivity is because her team members are engaged. Jessica says, "I am a believer that no one wants to come to a workplace that sucks. That's just human nature. People want to do their best. They want to be here. When you make it fun, when you trust them because they are part of a team, and you appreciate your teammates, they'll prove you right and will exceed your expectations ten times over."

Employee recognition programs play a vital role in creating a workplace culture that ROCKS. They are even more critical during times of crisis and uncertainty (like the COVID pandemic). So, why is it so important to recognize your employees? Because surveys show that 69% of employees reveal they would work harder if their managers recognized their efforts more often. By addressing your employees' wants and needs and aligning them with your company values, your recognition efforts positively impact your company's bottom line.

There are lots of numbers to support engagement efforts. For example, did you know that 78% of employees are highly engaged when they feel strong recognition from their leaders, compared to 34% of highly engaged employees in companies with weak recognition programs? But unfortunately, only 1 out of 5 employees strongly agree their leaders manage performance in a way that motivates them to do outstanding work.

Here are a few more statistics to support you in justifying the benefits of an employee engagement program:

- LinkedIn found that 69% of employees will work harder if their efforts are more frequently recognized. They also discovered that 80% of Millennials prefer on-the-spot recognition over formal performance reviews.
- Gallup reports that workers who are not adequately recognized are 2x more likely to leave next year.
- Glassdoor found that 53% of employees would stay at their jobs longer if they felt more appreciated by their employer.
- Qualtrics says that employees who have managers who regularly acknowledge them for good work are five times more likely to stay
- The Harvard School of Public Policy found companies with peer-to-peer recognition are 35% more likely to report lower turnover
- Companies with service award programs retain employees for 2-4 more years than companies without a service award program.

When it comes to recognition programs, there is no one-size-fits-all approach. What sounds suitable for one company may not work for yours. Whatever you choose to do, your program should be comprehensive, and all feedback given to employees should be authentic, relevant, and specific.

There are three key types of recognition, all of which serve different purposes:

Microrecognition includes things you can do fairly quickly and easily to recognize staff. It may consist of sending notes, giving gift cards, posting on bulletin boards – anything frequent and ongoing.

Informal recognition: Holding a pizza party, potluck, or a happy hour to celebrate a milestone anniversary, a goal achievement, or project completion is a great way to put some fun into your recognition program. Informal recognition occurs more spontaneously and changes often.

Formal recognition is more structured. These programs typically require planning, a large budget, a nomination or selection process, and a ceremony or special event.

No matter what program you choose, the only prerequisite is to be meaningful for your employees. Recognition is most effective when provided regularly and shared at the moment.

Acknowledge employees specifically for the excellent work they do. Tell your staff why you are thankful for them and how their actions impact you and the company. It's easy to hold off on sharing it for various reasons, but there is no good reason you should wait to thank an employee for their hard work. Make recognition a part of your culture.

You'll want to use various types of recognition to keep things fresh and fun. One kind of recognition may be great for a while, and then it gets old. Always look for ways to kick it up a notch. You can improve your program by finding out how your employees like to be acknowledged. Some staff may not want public recognition during company meetings, but they save every note or card you give them. Make sure your praise is genuine and back it up with specifics. Let them know what they did to support you - whether it's crushing a project or going above and beyond to delight customers.

It's important to note that acknowledgment doesn't always have to come from the leadership. When employees are recognized by their peers, it is 35% more likely to have a positive impact on their employee experience than getting recognized by their manager alone. One effective practice is to throw your employees' names into a hat each time they recognize one of their colleagues. Don't limit the number of entries awarded. Pick a couple of names from the hat at the end of the week and let those employees enjoy a prize.

It's also nice to share your appreciation of your employees with the rest of the world on social media. Social recognition is a great way to spread the word about how proud you are of your team. This practice also helps build your employer brand and can help attract new talent to your organization. In addition, most employees who receive a public acknowledgment from their boss are more likely to share those posts with their friends and followers, creating brand ambassadors who represent your organization well.

Please note: before posting on social media, make sure your employees know what you're planning to share and are okay with being recognized publicly first. After all, not everyone wants to be in the public spotlight; some employees would rather receive their praise behind closed doors!

Birthday cakes and parties are certainly an excellent way to celebrate employees' special days. However, giving them the day off to do what they please will take your celebration to a whole new level. If a day off doesn't work with your company policy, you can personalize birthday celebrations by decorating an employee's desk and presenting them with their favorite dessert.

Also, don't forget the card! Giving your team members tangible evidence of your appreciation with a card signed by their colleagues creates a more meaningful experience. It also gives each team member the chance to personally let the birthday person know why they are thankful for them. For your remote staff, you may want to record a video of everyone wishing them well and then mail a cake and a thoughtful gift to their address to share the love.

When you tell someone you appreciate them, you create a beautiful memory. When you give them a handwritten note, you create a treasure. Leaving a Post-It note on your employee's desk as a thank you creates a meaningful moment for the recipient. When you acknowledge your employees for specific actions, you also promote repeated behaviors and encourage the growth of solid company culture.

Have some fun with your recognition program. Maybe you can find a trophy, stuffed animal, or other knick-knacks that you can pass around the office. When you give it to an employee who went above and beyond, they get to keep the item for a week on their desk – then it's up to them to find the next person to bestow the honor upon. This is a great way to encourage peer-to-peer recognition and build a culture of recognition. Make gratitude a priority in your company by keeping it top of mind for everyone in the organization.

Remember that Employee Appreciation Day is held on the first Friday of March each year. It's the perfect opportunity to show your employees how much they mean to you. You may want to extend the event to be celebrated all week with food, team-building activities, contests, and wellness activities. Have some special planned for each day – perhaps one day for chair massages, another day for a costume party, or bring in food trucks for a yummy meal.

A simple way to make appreciation a regular part of your company culture is to start each meeting by sharing team wins, good news, and thank you's. For example, if an employee closed a huge account, or completes a project, encourage them to share the announcement at the beginning of a meeting.

You can also recognize your employees' strengths by inviting them to participate in a project, join a culture committee, or give them professional development opportunities so they can try new things to build their skills. You can also let your employees participate in a hackathon. Let them take a whole or half-day to work on a project of their choosing, either in groups or on their own. At the end of the day, have participants present their idea before the leadership team and implement the top ideas into the day-to-day operations.

A Gallup workplace survey noted the types of recognition employees find most memorable. The top five are:

- Public recognition
- Private recognition from a boss, peer, or customer
- Receiving a high level of achievement through evaluations
- Promotion or increase in scope and responsibility
- Monetary awards pay increase, trips, etc.

Notice that the top two memorable forms of recognition have very little to do with money. Of course, money is essential, but it's not the number one (or number two) top way to recognize team members.

One of the best and easiest ways to get started is to create an employee "all about me" sheet. First, survey your employees to find out their favorite candy bar, gift card, restaurant, hobby, sports team, etc. Then, when that person goes above and beyond, and you want to recognize them at the moment, you can do so with something that you know that they like.

The nice thing about the All About Me sheet is that the employee may not even remember filling it out. Still, when you acknowledge them with their favorite candy bar, there's something in their subconscious mind that will say, "Wow, they're paying attention to me."

Recognition: Action Ideas

Individuals:

1. Be more vocal in your appreciation efforts. Let your colleagues know that you appreciate them and be specific in your accolades.
2. Set a goal to thank at least one person every day. Especially look for behind-the-scenes people who don't get acknowledged often. You'll make their day.
3. Remember that everyone likes to be appreciated – including the boss. So, if you enjoy working for your manager, let them know precisely what they do well.

Management:

1. Start your meetings by allowing people to share thirty seconds of good news. It can be personal or professional. You may also include some time for people to thank and acknowledge each other – and spend time in "kudos review."

2. Give your employees some time to catch up by having a "no meetings day." You may find they'll be much more productive without so many distractions.
3. Allow employees to finish up and leave early on the day before a holiday weekend. Even a 30-minute head start will help with rush hour traffic and make their day - and weekend - even better.

Organization:

1. Put in a suggestion box - and a digital version for remote employees. Let employees remain anonymous if they'd like and give credit to employees whose ideas you implement.
2. Rework your employees' schedules to allow for more flexibility. Time is the greatest gift you can give most of your team members.
3. In addition to your micro- and informal recognition practices, consider going all out for a formal recognition event. Allow employees to bring their spouse/significant other to celebrate the occasion with them.

Engage Your Employees Through Ethics, Internships, and Flextime:
Case Study: Win-Tech

"In matters of style, swim with the current; in matters of principle, stand like a rock."
~ **Thomas Jefferson**

Allison Giddens began her career with a large media conglomerate. Although she learned a lot while there, her biggest lesson was that a corporate job was not for her. While pet sitting for Dennis, a neighbor who owned a small business, she told him, "I want to come work for you." He replied, "You don't even know what I do." She said, "I said I don't care. I know it's a small business, and I want to get involved in that."

Dennis interviewed Allison and brought her on board as an administrative assistant. It wasn't long before she set her sights on bigger and better projects within this small manufacturing company. As Operations Director, Allison realized that in the thirty-year Win-Tech history, no one had purposely gone out of their way to figure out what the company's core values were. It felt like their culture was driving them rather than the other way around.

Allison knew that an essential component of building a solid organization was discovering its core values and building its culture around them.

Allison asked Dennis to write down fifty adjectives that meant something to him and the values he attributed to Win-Tech to get started with this project. Dennis is a man of few words, so it was initially tough to pull out fifty adjectives. But, once Allison had the list, she went back to the employees and said, "Okay, here are 50 adjectives. What do you think we're missing from Win-Tech's essential values?"

Initially, Allison thought that employees would be uninterested in the value-defining process. However, the idea gained steam, and employees enthusiastically participated in the project. Through numerous conversations and Survey Monkey results, three words rose to the top that employees felt held the most significant value and set Win-Tech apart from other organizations. Those words were accuracy, respect, and accountability.

Accuracy was a given. After all, Win-Tech is a manufacturing company, and its work needs to be accurate. By focusing on precision, employees realized that their actions made a difference each day, and they constantly looked for new and better ways to improve their work processes.

Accountability. You can't hold people responsible if you don't set expectations for them. One of the ways Allison implemented more responsibility in the plant was to initiate five-minute stand-up meetings every Tuesday afternoon. Allison recalls that it was a little more challenging to get 30 people together and keep them six feet apart when dealing with the pandemic, but they made it happen. In doing so, they could communicate the same thing to everybody simultaneously.

Respect ultimately speaks to the importance of integrity that employees find imperative. Focusing on these specific terms has led to better communication within the team.

The company owner, Dennis Winslow, was an excellent example of showing respect for his team members. He was the first to pick up the broom and sweep the shop floor. He also expected the same commitment to excellence from his management team. By evening the playing field and getting rid of the "us versus them" feeling between employees and leadership made a huge difference in the culture. When you roll up your sleeves and get involved in the day-to-day work alongside your employees, they notice.

Besides defining their company values, Allison knew that it was essential to attract and recruit new employees to their company. Their initial plan was to bring a couple of high school students onto the shop floor to participate in a project. Then the world got turned upside down with the pandemic. So instead of canceling on those students, she created a 15-day internship program.

Allison invited a group of industry professionals to dial in and gave the students insight into their professions within the industry. They looked at everything, including supply chain, accounting, marketing, shop floor, metallurgy. Then, they had subject matter experts speak to the students for about 30 or 40 minutes. At the end of the program, the students gave a presentation to summarize what they had learned.

Not only did they get a wide breadth of manufacturing expertise thrown at them, but they also created their own network. The subject matter experts kept in touch, and it was an excellent opportunity for both parties. Finally, Win-Tech, Inc. changed its hours in August 2021 to a four-day workweek.

Allison is doing things right at Win-Tech. By getting the employees involved in figuring out the words that described their culture, she achieved a much stronger buy-in than if she had left it up to the management team alone.

Allison found a unique way to introduce Win-Tech and the manufacturing industry to students as career options through an internship program. By involving local experts, she gave the experts the chance to give back to their community, and she also gave the students introductions to people who could help and support them in their career journey.

By rethinking her plant's scheduling and going to a four-day workweek, she gave her employees the one gift that we all have the same amount of, and yet we never seem to have enough of – she gave them their time back. Not only did she adjust the schedule, but she also offered learning opportunities for employees to develop their skills to grow in their careers. She also gave tenured employees, like her machinist, opportunities to help and support others and build relationships along the way.

Reflection questions:

1. If you were to compile a shortlist of your company's values and ethics, what would they be? Would your employees agree?
2. How can you get involved with your local community – tech schools, community colleges, etc. – to attract more people into your industry?
3. In what ways can you look at your working hours and schedule differently? In what areas can you add flexibility and give your team members some of their time back?

Train Your Leaders Well to Increase Retention

"Corporate culture matters. How management chooses to treat its people impacts everything—for better or for worse."
~ Simon Sinek

You've probably been hearing about employee engagement for years. But really, why should you care about it? Two words: engagement matters. Many statistics show how companies with engaged employees have 41% lower absenteeism and 21% better profitability. In addition, engaged employees are 87% less likely to leave than their disengaged counterparts. So, here's the bottom line: you can make more money, be more profitable, and spend less time hiring and training new employees if you create the right type of work culture. And your culture starts with your leadership team.

Take a minute and think back to the "The one that got away." You know the one — that employee with you since the beginning. You knew them and their family. You depended on them through thick and thin. Then one day, they just left. What happened? You thought things were great, and then, your most loyal, long-term employee, the one that's been with you forever, goes and takes another job for slightly more money.

Many business owners are so focused on the product, the services, and the day-to-day running of the business that they don't even think about asking their employees how they're doing and how they can help them. Maybe those managers believe that if employees weren't okay, they would say something. Or perhaps they don't have the personal skills to help their team members feel safe sharing what's really going on.

You work so hard and spend lots of time, energy, and money finding the right people for your team. So, it's frustrating when they leave. Although nothing will guarantee that your people will NEVER leave you, paying attention to their engagement levels may encourage them to stay. Starting with your managers is an excellent way to see results.

Please understand that it is not your responsibility to fulfill all your employees' needs all the time. (That should bring a sigh of relief!) You do, however, want to create the type of culture that makes people want to work harder and bring more value than what you're paying them. Changing your workplace culture can only be accomplished if your entire management team is on board. If you're unable to get the buy-in you need from your managers, you may have to rethink their role within your company.

Take a moment to consider how you and your leadership team show up at work. Here's the thing, the best leaders do more than show up. They are approachable. They know about their employees' families, about what they like to do. Their employees feel respected. They feel that management appreciates their efforts.

One good way to figure out how you're showing up is to pay attention to what happens when you walk into the room. Do people clam up or continue what they're doing? Do employees smile and say "hello," or do they look concerned and avoid eye contact? There's an old saying that some people light up the room when they walk in, and others light up the room when they leave. As a manager or as a leader in your organization, you're the one that sets that precedent. So again - your company's culture starts with you.

As you walk through your building, make sure to greet people and make eye contact while doing it. Then, ask how they're doing. Call them by their name, perhaps ask them about their kids, spouse, family, etc. Put aside all those thoughts of everything you have on your plate and all the work you need to do. Every interaction you have with a team member creates a moment. Those moments can be positive, or they may be negative. If you choose to take out your nasty mood on an employee, even if it's just one time, you could be damaging that relationship from that day forward.

Here's an example of what can happen. You're stressed out and in a bad mood one day. You snap at one of your employees. You didn't know it, but that person had been thinking about leaving. Maybe they have an offer for another job. Perhaps they want a change of scenery. That offhand comment may be the final straw that makes that employee say, "That's it, I'm out of here." You've lost them.

On the other hand, if you notice that an employee is having a bad day and you ask how you can help, you may turn around their decision to leave your organization. Instead, they remind themself, "You know, I have it pretty good here. I'm going to stay."

So how you show up each day is how your employees perceive you. It's how they react to you when you're walking through the building. Are you there to make their lives and their days a little bit better, or do they know that because you're there, their day and their life will be just a little bit worse?

Conversely, if you're neither making their day better nor worse, it could suggest a lack of leadership presence and influence, which is also unproductive for everyone around. An absent leader or someone who feels out of touch with their employees does not drive employee engagement either.

Everything does not have to be "happy, happy, joy, joy" all the time. But if 90% of the time your employees know that you're coming at them from a place of positivity and you regularly catch them in the act of doing things well, they are more likely to know, like, and trust you. When they respect you, the occasional "off" day is forgivable. But for the most part, if you don't have that level of connection with them, then the chance of you engaging and keeping your employees goes way down.

You may think, "This is just the way I am. I can't change. My employees are just going to have to live with it." The fact is that there are people who are naturally better at leading people than others. There is an inherent personality trait where people are connectors. If you look at things like Strengths Finders" by Tom Rath, you'll discover characteristics like WOO – which is "winning others over." For WOO people, it's a little easier because they are natural connectors. Other people must work a little harder at it. If this doesn't come naturally to you, step out of your comfort zone and try something new.

Unfortunately, what often happens is that managers treat their employees the way their former boss treated them. So, for example, you worked for a boss who never praised you or said, "thank you." Perhaps a boss berated you when things didn't go well and never said anything nice to you. If any of these situations happened to you, there's a good chance that you will treat your employees the same way. But, on the other hand, take a moment and reflect on a boss you respected in your career. How did their behavior impact your confidence, enjoyment, and motivation in your job? How can you do the same for your people?

Much research has been done around personality types. Consider, for example, a leader who is a "Dominant" personality type on the DiSC assessment (extroverted/task-oriented). These leaders may need to learn to adapt their communication style not to polarize their staff who are wired differently (Influence, Steadiness, and Consciousness types). Some staff members may not take well to their natural style, whereas other Dominants may be okay with it. Diversity in personality types is critical but requires adaptive communication styles from people managers.

And for the leaders who are "wired" as an introvert or don't see things from the "people" point of view, they may have a more difficult time communicating with their extroverted team members. So, leaders need to understand themselves better and strive to understand better the people they work with every day. It makes a world of difference when you can talk to people in a way that works for them.

Think about your most introverted engineer or accountant and your most extroverted sales rep or customer service person. Unless they've been working together forever, those two people probably have difficulty talking to each other. So, if you're thinking that this sounds like a bunch of that psychobabble, soft skill stuff and you've heard it all before, please know that if you implement a few simple strategies, you WILL see the results.

Although these skills are often referred to as "soft skills," there is nothing soft about them. On the contrary, they are "essential skills." For example, suppose you're a numbers person. In that case, developing your leadership skills will help your productivity numbers grow, your absenteeism levels lower, you'll have greater profitability, as well as more significant commitment and loyalty to your organization. All this is because your employees feel connected to you, and you make it hard for them to go somewhere else – even if you're not the highest paying employer in your area.

Look to create a learning culture in your organization. Giving employees at all levels opportunities to learn gives you a huge bang for your buck. Of course, you need to have training and development resources in-house, but sending your new supervisors to outside training may also make a huge difference.

Think about it, when you promote your best hourly employee to a supervisor, you've potentially just made them your worst manager if they don't have the training they need to succeed. All you need to do is watch a couple of episodes of Undercover Boss, and you'll see all kinds of examples of management "fails." Suppose you're not familiar with Undercover Boss. In that case, it's a reality show where the owner or top leader goes undercover in their organization to see what's really going on in their company. Then, they roll up their sleeves and do the "dirty work" that their employees must deal with every day. By the end of the show, that leader has an entirely different perspective of their employees and business. One of the most common fixes they implement is a new training program. Why? Because it works.

When you promote an employee into management, they may be terrified to ask questions because they're thinking, "Well, I just got this promotion. If I ask this question, they're going to think I'm not as talented as they thought, and maybe my manager will wonder why they promoted me." When you send them off-site to new supervisor training, they're with other people who are in the same boat. Now they don't feel so alone.

You're also allowing them to try out new skills in a safe place. Don't forget that when they come back from that training, make a point to sit down and debrief them about what they learned and what skills they can use to put the training into practice every day. In your conversation, ask them, "How can I help you? What did you learn? What tools do you need to implement it? How can I support you?" Finally, when you send employees to training for a couple of days, schedule a review conversation surrounding the training session. If you don't, there is a strong chance that all that newly learned information will go out the window, and you will feel you just wasted training dollars.

According to the research done by the Society for Human Resource Management, 84% of U.S. workers report that poorly trained managers create a lot of unnecessary work and stress. Additionally, 57% of American employees feel their managers would benefit from "soft skills" training on being a better manager. These workers believe that their performance would improve if the training helped.

The top skills people would like to see their managers improve are:

- Communicating effectively
- Developing and training the team
- Managing time and delegating
- Cultivating a positive and inclusive team culture
- Managing team performance

Train Your Leaders: Action ideas:

Individuals:

1. Seek out opportunities for personal and professional development. Whether you sign up for online classes at your local community college, go to a public seminar, or enroll in an online course in a topic of interest to you, focus on your areas of interest first and then expand to other topics outside your comfort zone.

2. When you go to training, share what you learned with your manager. You'll let them know that their investment in you is paying off. Look for ways to implement at least one or two best practices.
3. Incorporate learning into your day. Even if you have a full plate, find ways to learn while in your daily routine. Listen to podcasts or audiobooks while driving. Set a goal to read five pages of a book each morning. Watch TED talks or other educational videos on YouTube when you have a few minutes of downtime. Little bits of effort throughout the week adds up over time.

Management:

1. When you have employees seeking out additional growth opportunities, find a way to provide those opportunities for them. Remember that no employee ever quits because of "too much training."
2. Put together a resource library and educate your managers and staff on using the resources. You may want to assign a few pages or a chapter to a team member and have them share the ideas they learned at your next meeting.
3. When you are in a training session, give it your full attention. Stop multitasking – don't check emails, take phone calls, or otherwise divert your attention from the shared information.
4. Ask employees about topics they would like to learn about and host occasional lunch and learn sessions so employees and managers can get together and have the same conversation about a topic. Keep in mind that lunch breaks for your remote employees are an important time for them to disconnect. In-person, lunch and learns bring people together. Virtual training keeps people potentially tied longer to their computers.

Organization:

1. Create a learning culture. Don't use training as punishment. Let your team members know that you are proud to invest in their growth and development.
2. If your company mindset is, "Why should we invest all this money in our people? They're just going to take that investment and leave anyway," turn that thought around and ask yourself, "So what happens if we don't invest in our people – and they STAY?"
3. Don't focus your training dollars only on new employees, managers, and high potentials. Expand your offerings to give development opportunities to all employees. Only a small percentage of them will take advantage of the training, and your future leaders may come from unexpected sources.

No Employee Ever Quit Because of Too Much Training

"The only thing worse than training employees and losing them is to not train them and keep them."
~Zig Ziglar

Leaders often offer training and development opportunities to managers, supervisors, and "high-potential" employees in their organization. But what about the rest of your team? Allison Giddens, President of Win-Tech, an aerospace machine shop, wanted to expand opportunities for professional development to her shop employees. After considering several alternatives based on employee feedback, she came up with a plan.

On the first Friday of each month, Allison makes computers available on the shop floor for people who want additional (self-led) training using training software and apps. The sign-ups started slowly, with only a few people taking advantage of the offer. But, when a more seasoned machinist came to see her, she knew she was on the right track. He not only took a few programs, but he also offered to be available in case anyone had questions that the training software couldn't answer.

Allison noticed that the people she expected to participate in the training did. However, she also saw people she didn't think interested in professional development take advantage of these opportunities. So instead of making judgments and focusing on those who she thought had the highest potential, she kept these opportunities open to everyone, and it's paying off big for her company's profitability, productivity levels, and retention rate.

According to ATD - the Association for Talent Development - companies spend an average of $1,267 each year per employee for training. You might be thinking, "If we invest all of that money in our people, they're probably just taking advantage of it and then leaving the company anyway." Well, here's something else to consider - what if you don't invest in them – and they stay?!!!

During my programs, I'll often ask audience members how they invest in their team members. One woman at an HR conference replied that her company gave every employee $1500 per year to invest in whatever personal or professional development they wanted. Even though that was higher than the average, audience members thought that company was being overly generous with their employees. They struggled to figure out how her company could afford to give so much money away. When asked how many people took advantage of this offer, surprisingly, she revealed that only about 3-5% of her employees took advantage of these training opportunities. But the ones who did? THEY became the organization's future leaders.

Before taking on any training program, your commitment to it is vital. Your leaders must see the long-term benefits and then support and promote them. If managers are not excited about the training program and fail to communicate its importance, your staff will not see the benefits. Often, employees may view training as "just another checklist item." Because managers and team leaders often have the most significant influence on their team members, leaders must also commit to the training's implementation.

Most employees don't quit their job because of "too much training." Not only is it essential for you to invest in your team, but you also want to make sure that you're doing it the right way. There are many "bright, shiny objects" available for training. Keep your employees up to speed on the latest developments while spending the time to understand how your team members work. Look at what's changing in their roles and how urgent this new training compares to other business priorities. This attention to your team members' preferences makes a massive difference in the value you receive from them.

If your training programs are not resonating, check to make sure that they are relevant to the issues and concerns of your employees. Every course is different, so make sure you choose one with current, helpful, and entertaining content. It's also good to track completion rates to show how the training affects productivity and engagement.

As your employees grow and develop in their knowledge and expertise, your company will also benefit. A recent study shows that companies see an 8.6% increase in productivity for every 10% increase in employee training and development. When you put pen to paper, you may discover the cost of training will pay for itself over time. Instead of looking at training to check a box or make sure everyone gains a specific skill, focus on the benefits of education to the organization.

Although employees may be responsible for completing online training on their own, it doesn't mean it must be an isolated activity. For example, managers may invite employees to talk about their courses at weekly team meetings. They can also assign a lesson to all team members then discuss it. Team learning keeps engagement levels high, ensures completion, and reinforces the concepts learned. In addition, these activities allow team members to stay connected even when working remotely.

Many companies are afraid to implement training programs because they think the employees will take the course to improve their skills and leave for better opportunities. Fortunately, in most cases, this doesn't happen. Instead, educating your employees increases retention and engagement while enhancing productivity and profitability. In addition, when you have a team of highly skilled employees, you also have access to a tremendous internal pipeline for internal promotions within your organization.

Investing in training to retain your employees is more cost-effective than hiring new team members. The greatest benefit? You'll have a skilled team who feels valued by you and are more likely to stay. Keep in mind that each of your employees learns differently and at a dissimilar pace. Even employees doing the same job often understand their roles in their own way. Recognize that your employees have unique learning styles.

Use a combination of online learning, in-person workshops, webinars, and mobile games to reinforce learning and increase knowledge retention. Recognizing the various learning styles and considering your employees' learning strengths and challenges will help you improve your professional development outcomes. When employees go the extra mile in their course completion activities, take the time to recognize and appreciate the effort they are giving you to enhance their skill levels.

You also want to provide proper training to your in-house course facilitators. Like everything else, the ability to train others is a learned skill. When employees are nervous or uncomfortable speaking to their peers, they probably won't perform at their peak. Offer a training "on-boarding" process to help your internal trainers identify different training methods and learning styles. Help your instructors feel at ease with the tech and the materials they'll use. Encourage them to shadow your top educators to see how practical training is done and help them get comfortable with their new training role.

When you put some thought into your training curriculum, the ROI on your investment will be measurable and will give your leadership team the results they are looking for. Here are a few ways you can invest in your staff.

Peer-to-Peer Training: Have your employees teach their coworkers a concept or skill. In doing so, you'll give team members visibility and respect from their colleagues and managers while offering a wide range of topics from which employees can learn.

Lunch and learns: Invite your staff to get together and learn something over lunch (or another meal). Here are a few ideas to get started:

1. Ask employees about topics they would like to learn – and don't hold them to strictly business topics. You want to get as many people interested in the subject as possible to build momentum for future lunch and learns.
2. Choose a video on YouTube, a training program from a vendor, or any other short lesson for employees to discuss. To make it fun, you may also allow employees to submit their ideas on a piece of paper, toss them into a hat, and select one of the topics at random.
3. Pick up the tab for lunch and let the employees learn while breaking bread with each other. The meal price is minimal compared to the value your staff will receive from this activity.

Learning library: Many of your employees haven't picked up a nonfiction book since high school or college. Instead of assuming they know how to properly use educational materials, assign them a specific chapter or topic. After having your employee read the given short section, ask them to share their thoughts and ideas on the subject. Offer access to a resource library to assist them in their professional growth as one of your company benefits. A robust career development program is a crucial criterion for many job seekers.

Ongoing training – in-house: Create a learning culture and encourage people to participate as often as possible. Pay them for hours they invest in personal and professional development to incentivize them to continue their education. Then, as they begin to experience the benefits of their newfound knowledge, they are more likely to continue learning independently.

Bring in a trainer: Your employees get to see you, your HR professionals, and your training team every day. They will hear and comprehend educational information differently when you bring in a new face to conduct training sessions. Outside trainers bring a unique perspective in their delivery because they are not pigeon-holed into your organization's way of thinking.

Public seminars: When you promote an employee to a supervisor position, you've potentially created your worst new supervisor if you don't give that person adequate training. Sending employees offsite for training helps them meet and network with others in the same position. They can then learn leadership skills in a safe environment and have opportunities to ask questions that they may be intimidated to ask their manager who just promoted them.

Trade shows: If your industry has local, regional, or national trade shows and conferences, make a point to bring employees with you. Don't just bring your leadership team; offer the opportunity to a variety of people in the organization. When your employees get to see first-hand what's going on in the market, the competition, and with their customers, they will better appreciate your industry and feel more connected to it. In addition, they feel valued by you because they realize you made a significant investment bringing them to the event.

It's essential that you don't look at training as punitive. Don't "send" people to training; instead, "invest" in them. Your employees will notice the difference in your wording. In today's employee-centered market, your company's reputation is everything. When you invest in your team members, you create a culture where employees feel valued and appreciated. When employees know their company provides for their career development, they are less likely to leave a negative review on websites like Glassdoor or Indeed. Training dollars are a small price to pay for the significant returns you will receive for your investment.

Investing in your people: Action Ideas:

Individuals:

1. Seek out opportunities for additional growth within your company. Be specific in your request and show your boss how these courses will help you in your job.
2. Invest in personal and professional development for yourself. Keep track of all the sessions that you've attended. Share that information with your manager during your performance review.
3. When you go to a training, share what you learned with your supervisor and look for ideas that you and your manager may implement.

Management:

1. Put pen to paper and figure out how much you currently invest in your employees' training and development. If the number is too low, look for ways to increase development opportunities for your team.
2. Survey employees to find out the kinds of development opportunities they are interested in pursuing. Don't limit them to job-specific skill-building courses.
3. Discover your employees' skills and talents and encourage them to lead training sessions that support their peers and colleagues. Give them a bonus or some other kind of recognition for sharing their knowledge with their coworkers.

Organization:

1. Commit to creating a learning environment and provide the resources your managers and employees need to get started. Invest in educational resources and house them in an area that is easily accessible by anyone who wants to use them.
2. Whatever the economy and the market are doing, commit to making your training budget one of the last items cut. You don't need to spend a lot of money on your development programs, but you want to keep the education process going.
3. Incentivize your employees to participate in training programs. You'll probably see that only a small percentage of your staff take advantage of the opportunities for further education. Keep your eye on those people. They are your future leaders.

How to Reboot Your Company Culture: Case Study: Karen Norheim, American Crane and Equipment Corporation

"Being a great place to work is the difference between being a good company and a great company."
~Brian Kristofek, President and CEO, Upshot

As President of American Crane and Equipment Corporation, Karen Norheim sought to solidify the company founder's legacy while putting her stamp on the company culture. So, in 2018, Karen and her leadership team decided to do a complete reboot, renaming their culture "Grit Matters." Focusing on perseverance, heart, and integrity, they worked on building their culture, cultivating their people, and nurturing their environment. This reboot became one of the key elements that helped them survive the Covid-19 pandemic two years later.

The leadership team started the reboot process by defining what made American Crane great and the essential factors to do even better. They revised their vision, mission, and core values statements and then did a rollout, which involved lots of communication with their team members.

Karen felt she communicated so much that she got tired of hearing herself talk. They held regular grit meetings, had grit contests, and gave grit bucks to highlight good grit behavior. They created postcards, logos, and stickers – doing everything they could do to get the word out and show their commitment to this culture change.

After a year of explaining and teaching their new grit philosophy, they were ready to go to phase two of integrating it into the organization's fabric. Finally, in December of 2019, they reached the tipping point. Employees got it, and everything was going well.

A few months later, Covid rocked their world. But because of their work over the last year, everyone stepped up. They realized how important it was for the company to keep up its business, despite the turbulence. So, they sent 1/3 of their workforce home (about 50+ people), including over 20 engineers with their workstations, to do a home setup on a Friday. Incredibly, they were all up and running and working, not skipping a beat, by the following week. Karen was proud of the flexibility and willingness to work together that her teammates showed. She believes her staff was the epitome of the difference between mediocrity and excellence.

When the pandemic was in full swing, Karen realized that she and her leadership team needed to communicate even more. So, they started with two videos per week and have since shifted to releasing a video every Monday. In addition, they have a Friday email and text messages with blog information to share what's happening: new orders, company news, and general thoughts.

Karen calls her process gardening. They're planting seeds, nurturing, growing, harvesting – and then they go back and plant again. It's a never-ending process, but her team gets it, and it feels good. Karen realizes that everyone wants to work in a place where they're appreciated. By making their people the most essential part of American Crane, she's created a fun workplace that cares about its employees and provides them with meaningful work.

Although Covid was a disruption, Karen feels it has added another competitive advantage. They let their customers know that they're gritty – they get things done. And in doing so, they continue to exceed their customer's expectations. They go the extra mile and handle challenging situations when things don't go according to plan. She prefers to look at failures as opportunities for learning moments.

Karen recommends being focused on your goal but flexible in your methods. Don't get so locked into doing things your exact way. Instead, give your people the pleasure of solving the problems and empowering them. You'll discover that when real success happens, it feels like magic. As a leader, you get to watch your people bring a project to fruition, and you know that it's all them, and it's all their own. There's a lot of pride that goes along with that.

When it all comes down to it, Karen believes that the pandemic strengthened them as a company. They had no choice but to empower their people, and Covid allowed them to throw everybody into this time of rapid change. Being in that uncomfortable space has led to amazing growth and the evolution of their people and company culture.

Reflection Questions:

1. Is my company culture working, or do we need a reboot? In what areas can we refresh our vision for the future?

2. How can we get our staff involved and support their buy into the process?
3. What fun, creative ways can we kick off a culture reboot? (Stickers, posters, meetings, contests, etc.)?
4. How can we adopt the "gardening" concept when working with our team? (Plant the seeds, nurture their development, harvest their good results, and start the process again.)

Keys to Onboarding Employees to Maximize Your ROI

"I truly believe that onboarding is an art. Each new employee brings with them the potential to achieve and succeed. To lose the energy of a new hire through poor onboarding is an opportunity lost."
~Sarah Wetzel, Director of Human Resources at engage: BDR

Dana Syndergaard is the HR Manager for CA Lawton, a fifth-generation foundry. Dana attributes Lawton's above-industry-average retention rate to its intensive onboarding process. Throughout their program, they create a sense of new hire safety and security that lasts throughout the employee's career.

Like most companies, CA Lawton has an orientation period. But what differentiates their program are the orientations after the initial orientation. New employees not only go through a company orientation, but they also go through safety, human resource, and continuous improvement orientations. They are introduced to the tasks they are required to do, and they take tests on their ability to complete those assignments. All along, they get regular feedback from their supervisors.

When Lawton initially implemented their onboarding program, they started with a two-week orientation. After discovering the need to spend more time acclimating new hires, they increased the onboarding period to three weeks and then to four weeks. During this period, new employees go through the process with a small core group of peers. The people in that core group tend to develop strong relationships. Because they build bonds with each other, it is more challenging for them to quit and go somewhere else. After all, they have friends in the facility.

Just in case you're not familiar with the term "onboarding," it is the process of introducing new hires to the company's policies, procedures, and culture. It's the first interaction a new hire has with their employer after their interview process; therefore, it must go well. If the experience fails to live up to the employees' expectations, they may regret accepting the job offer and quit quickly. With the ROI of employee onboarding estimated at $6,044 - $11,799 per new employee, effective onboarding directly impacts the bottom line, including productivity, profitability, and retention rates.

The onboarding process starts with preboarding. Preboarding is the time between offer acceptance and the employee's first day on the job. Because other interested parties may still be contacting your candidate, if they don't hear anything from you until the day they start, your new hire may wonder if they've made the right decision to join your organization. Unfortunately, radio silence during this critical time can mean losing the talent you've worked so hard to recruit.

Given that 58 percent of organizations admit their onboarding program focuses strictly on processes and paperwork, it is no surprise that many new employees leave their job within 90 days of starting because of these disappointing practices. On the other hand, a solid onboarding process helps new hires settle into their roles as they get to know the organization, obtain clarity on their job responsibilities, and build strong relationships with other team members. In addition, a positive onboarding experience makes employees feel welcome and helps them gel with their colleagues faster.

Sure, some HR managers still consider employee onboarding as simply the process where new hires fill out the paperwork. However, savvier HR professionals have a different perspective on the importance of the onboarding process. These HR leaders consider onboarding as the entire period beginning with the job offer and ending when the employee starts genuinely producing in their role.

If you're not holding onto new hires as long as you would like, reassessing your employee onboarding program is essential. After all, the first impression you create with your onboarding program can increase retention by 25% and improve employee performance by 11%. In addition, it's interesting to note that employees who participate in a structured onboarding program are 69% more likely to stay with their company for at least three years.

While it takes 8-12 months for new hires to be as proficient as their tenured colleagues, 15% of new employees shared that the lack of an effective onboarding program played a significant role in their early quitting decision.

Here are some ideas to include in your onboarding program:

1. Offer online new hire orientation before the employee's start date, so their first day can be about meaningful introductions, early learning, and creating a welcoming environment.
2. As you take them on a tour of the office, give your new hires the chance to look around and ask any questions they have about your

office culture and policies. Introduce them to everyone you meet and show them the spaces they're likely to access every day.
3. Make sure your onboarding process reflects your company's mission, values, and culture. Then, have some fun with it and make sure that the first day is enjoyable and memorable.
4. Send a thank you note or email along with a welcome email that includes all the information they need about your company and the job opportunity they now have with you.
5. Send regular communications in a variety of modes. Ask your new employee how they prefer to be contacted.
6. Provide skills training and offer personal support and encouragement. Look at mistakes as learning opportunities and if the errors are not a big deal, let them go.
7. Observe your employees as they do their tasks to see how you can help. Pay attention to how effectively you are communicating their roles and responsibilities.
8. Complete 1-week, 30-day, and 60-day quick check-ins to determine how the job is going overall and if employees have the specific support, resources, and equipment to do their work efficiently and effectively.

Here's a one-year onboarding checklist you can use or modify as necessary:

Day One:

Set expectations, introduce objectives, and make the employee feel comfortable in their new work environment. Make sure you set up their computer, confirm their business cards are ready and make sure it's evident that you were expecting them. Arrange for a "lunch buddy" to join them for a meal.

Point out the restrooms, break areas, kitchen, storage rooms, offices, and anything relevant to their day-to-day duties. Let them know where they can put their personal belongings and access work materials. Give them the access they need - keys, security codes, computer access, phone setup, and relevant training. Take some time to let them know how their job fits into the bigger picture for the company. Review policies for time off, sick time, holidays, vacation, etc.

Week One:

Have your tenured employees check in with the new team member to ensure they feel supported. Set realistic goals for the first week, month, 90-days, etc. Schedule weekly or bi-weekly meetings where you can connect with them one-on-one, provide feedback, and answer any questions.

Month One:

Review their first-month performance and provide any necessary coaching. Ensure their payroll is correct and any PTO accrual is functioning correctly. Check-in to make sure they are making adequate progress and set month-two goals to challenge them.

3-Month Check-in:

Determine any supplemental training needed. Review all metrics from the last ninety days and measure them against the goals you've set for them. Establish new goals for the next quarter, and switch to a quarterly check-in. Ask them how you're doing as a manager in supporting them. Find out which colleagues have been most helpful and ask for their suggestions for improving the onboarding process.

6-Month Check-In:

Review last quarter's goals and provide coaching where necessary. Add additional duties if they're ready and willing to take them on. Invite them to help in training any new hires. Set new goals for the next quarter and schedule their next quarterly check-in.

9-Month Check-In:

Review their goals and set new ones. Uncover any coaching opportunities and set the expectations for their annual review.

First-Year Check-In:

By now, your employee should have a firm grasp of the company's culture and goals. Assess their performance and celebrate their successes. Plan for career opportunities they may want to strive to attain. Set goals and learning opportunities for the year ahead.

An effective onboarding process helps you actively engage your employees so they can be productive on day one and build a successful, long-term career with your organization.

Onboarding: Action Ideas:

Individuals:

1. Be as low maintenance as possible on your first couple of days. Your boss and colleagues already have a lot on their plate, so don't add to their stress if a few minor things go wrong.
2. Smile, be kind and be approachable as you meet your new colleagues.
3. List all the reasons you decided to join your new company. It will affirm your decision and help deflect any "buyer's remorse."

Management:

1. Make your new hire's first day memorable by holding a "welcome" event. Let them meet the people they will be working with in a relaxed environment.
2. Assign new employees a "First 90 Days" partner. By giving new hires a go-to buddy who has been in the organization longer, they have a resource for questions, clarification, and friendly conversation.
3. As much as possible, customize the onboarding plan for each new hire. Set up required reading and scheduled times for meeting people and shadowing others.

Organization:

1. Have a member of upper management meet with each new hire, at least for a few minutes. You'll make that person feel extra special when they have access to top leaders.
2. Provide the resources and establish the relationships essential to new employees' understanding of your organization's written and unwritten norms.
3. Read and respond to onsite reviews on websites like Glassdoor.com. If you ignore these comments, you may dissuade new employees from filling out an application in the first place.

The Exit Interview May be Too Late, Try a Stay Interview Instead

"Employees who believe that management is concerned about them as a whole person – not just an employee – are more productive, more satisfied, more fulfilled. Satisfied employees mean satisfied customers, which leads to profitability."
~Anne M. Mulcahy

While speaking to the Industrial Fastener Institute a few years ago, I met Manny DeSantis, President of Valley Fastener Group. The story Manny shared during that program still sticks with me. It was an excellent example of a CEO putting himself out there to discover where his employees were coming from and how he could help. In addition, his stay interview process created a safe environment for all employees to share their thoughts, ideas, and suggestions without fear of reprisal.

Manny oversees three plants. Like an un-filmed episode of Undercover Boss, Manny wanted to know what was happening in his organization. So instead of putting on a disguise, he decided to meet with every employee one-on-one and ask them questions about their experience working at the company.

During the first round, the employees were unsure of his motives and, for the most part, gave him the answers they thought he wanted to hear. However, he did receive some ideas for improvement, and he proceeded to act on those suggestions. Employees saw that he was working on their behalf, and their trust grew.

The second round of interviews took place the following year, and employees were much more forthright with their feedback. Some of it was painful to hear, but Manny felt he was on the right track in building trust with his team. He continued to listen to his people without judgment, and slowly but surely, the culture started to change.

After several iterations of stay interviews, Manny has built strong relationships with his employees and his leadership team. While many CEOs spend their time in their office taking care of the day-to-day business issues, Manny takes the initiative to connect with his team – and the company is better off because of it.

So, what exactly is a stay interview? The stay interview is a scheduled conversation that a company leader, like Manny, uses to build trust with employees and assess their degree of satisfaction and engagement in the organization.

In most cases, it's the employee's direct manager who conducts the stay interview because they are the person who can most readily impact their staff's daily working conditions. In addition, these conversations stimulate the employee commitment to the organization because they are excited that their company's leadership is concerned enough about their future that their manager took the time to speak with them.

Most of the stay interview focuses on identifying and reinforcing the positive factors about the employee's job. Although the interviewer may cover some negative aspects, these questions are not the primary focus of the interview. The nice thing is that stay interviews don't require formal training.

A simple "how-to toolkit" or a list of questions is generally all a manager needs to successfully conduct these interviews. Stay interviews are usually inexpensive and informal. In most cases, the only major cost factors are thirty minutes to an hour of a manager's and an employee's time.

The stay interview's purpose is three-fold:

1. The manager wants to learn what their employees enjoy.
2. It helps leaders figure out what employees dislike about their job and the company.
3. It reinforces two-way communication between managers and their staff, creating a safe space for thoughts and feedback.

During stay interviews, managers ask their current employees for input using standard, structured questions to determine what people like about working there. Questions also uncover any grievances employees have that could compel them to look elsewhere for employment. Stay interviews also encourage employees to identify actions to improve their employee experience and eliminate their frustrations or turnover triggers.

When employees were asked about the most critical factors in their career during stay interview, 37 percent of respondents said that they valued recognition above all else. Discovering this information helps you understand how essential your employee recognition program is. It also helps you identify ways to acknowledge your team members. If you want to keep people around, it's crucial to recognize them in a way that resonates with them.

While employee recognition is important, employees also frequently mention that work-life balance is a huge reason they stay with their company. Companies that provide their staff with a healthy work-life balance are 25 percent more likely to retain them. If team members have to regularly come in early, stay late, and work into the wee hours of the morning, you may want to consider ways to improve their work-life balance before you lose your top people. A work-from-home policy that offers more flexibility may be just what your employees are seeking to stay with you.

Most companies are at least familiar with an exit interview. Many firms use exit interviews to find out why employees leave their jobs. Unfortunately, asking an employee on their last day, "why are you leaving?" doesn't provide the valuable information needed to prevent the turnover in the first place. By the time managers find out why employees are leaving, they cannot identify and solve the problems for the exiting employee.

Stay interviews deal with current employee feelings and issues, while exit interviews occur while the former employee is already walking out the door. Although employee satisfaction surveys help get some current information, stay interviews are more effective because they consist of dialogue where an employee can ask questions and follow up on their ideas.

Not all organizations are ripe for stay interviews. For example, if your organization lacks trust and is not good with open and honest communication and feedback, stay interviews are probably not for you. On the other hand, if you're unsure about how to start, an anonymous satisfaction survey may be the best way for you to begin to collect the information you need to change your workplace culture. However, suppose your company actively encourages open communication and employee involvement. In that case, these interviews can give you the feedback you need to keep a positive culture and attract new employees to join you.

How often should you hold stay interviews? You'll want to conduct your stay interviews at specific times and during fixed intervals. Some ideas include:

Three months after onboarding: Because the turnover rate of new employees tends to be higher than for more established employees, you may want to conduct a stay interview relatively soon after their onboarding to retain them for longer.

Six months after onboarding: Have a follow-up interview with new employees after about six months to reduce turnover rates further. This interview also allows you to address issues before they escalate or negatively impact the employee.

Once a year: Holding one stay interview per year will generally give you the feedback you want. Just make sure you schedule the interviews separately from your formal performance reviews.

Keep in mind that if you choose to conduct stay interviews, you must commit to making positive changes. Otherwise, it's an exercise in frustration for your staff. You may not be able to act on all the ideas and suggestions gained from your conversations, but letting employees know what happened due to the interactions makes for a much more impactful interview.

You want to make sure you stay away from a few things in a stay interview. Don't ask yes-or-no and closed-ended questions. Avoid asking your employees questions like, "Are you happy working here?" or "Do you make enough money?" Don't lead employees to believe that you can do things you can't do for them.

Here are some questions to choose from to design your stay interview:

- What makes you most happy at work?
- What do you look forward to every day at work?
- What career goals are most important to you?
- What keeps you working here?
- How do you like to be recognized?
- How could we support you better?
- What would make your job more satisfying?
- Do you feel fully utilized in your current role?
- How can we improve as a company and as a leadership team?
- What would you change about our company culture?
- What's holding you back from doing what you love to do?
- Are you doing the job you want to do?
- What can I do better as your manager?
- What would make you consider leaving?
- What can I do to better support you?
- How do you want to do your job?
- What do you like most or least about working here?
- What keeps you working here?
- If you could change something about your job, what would that be?
- What talents are you not using in your current role?
- Talk about a day that caused you anxiety or frustration?
- Within the past year, what was a "good day"?
- What does your dream job look like?
- What did you love about the last position that you no longer have?
- What do you think about on your way to work?
- What do you think about on your way home from work?
- What have you felt good about accomplishing in your job and your time here?
- What can I do to make your experience better?

- What kind of feedback about your performance or recognition would you like that you aren't currently receiving?
- What opportunities for self-improvement would you like to have that go beyond your current role?"

Stay interview Action Ideas:

Individuals:

1. When your manager meets with you for a stay interview, share your answers openly and honestly while maintaining respect for the interviewer.
2. Propose realistic and practical changes that you think may be possible for your employer or manager to implement.
3. View your stay interview as a way to engage in ongoing dialogue with management. Use it to improve your workplace by working together as a team.

Management:

Before doubling down on what you think your employees want, take the time to gather their feedback during a stay interview.

1. Go into the interview with a "thank you for sharing" attitude. Do not argue or justify anything about the organization.
2. Listen 80% of the time. Although this is a dialogue, your employee should do most of the talking.
3. During the interview, pause and give your employees time to think through their responses.

Organization:

1. Commit to positive change based on the answers you receive from your staff.
2. Give credit where credit is due, so employees know that you act on their ideas.
3. Based on the answers received, generate a list of actions your company could take to improve employee morale, engagement, and retention.

How to Express Gratitude in a Remote Workplace: Case Study: Paul McEwan, Rea & Associates

"Silent gratitude isn't very much to anyone."
Gertrude Stein, novelist

Paul McEwan is a principal at Rea & Associates. He's always been a big believer in the power of gratitude, and he makes a point to infuse appreciation into everything they do at Rea. They have a strategic plan called The Rea Advantage, which contains four cornerstones - People, Clients, Growth, and the Firm. Paul believes that these cornerstones are in the correct order. By focusing on their people first, everything else falls into place.

To demonstrate how important these concepts of gratitude and the four cornerstones are to him, Paul includes them in the signature line of his emails, and he models the values in all team meetings and discussions.

Paul believes that company culture is a reflection of the tone at the top, and it's essential to hire people who fit the culture's mold that sets them up for success. They used to hire people with the right background and technical expertise but didn't necessarily hold these team values. They believed they could change that person – and they found it didn't work. Now they look for people with these personal skills and attitudes and train them on the technical aspects of the job. It's all about hiring the person that fits best on the team, and teaching them how to do what Rea needs them to do.

The interesting thing about Paul's team is that they are primarily remote and have been that way since before the pandemic. Nobody is supervising anyone on a day-to-day basis. Instead, they assume their people are doing their jobs and have built a high trust work environment. Offering a remote option has been an excellent way to recruit new employees, especially women. Their employees like the flexibility - whether they've got kids or elderly parents that they're trying to take care of at home, flexibility is important.

Paul feels that they pioneered the remote workplace at Rea. They've always had it as an option, but when Covid came along, and everyone got sent home, they had more people take advantage of it. They do have a hybrid option. For example, Paul works in the office three days a week and is home two days a week.

They have had quite a bit of success onboarding new people into a completely remote environment, primarily using Zoom with a lot of screen sharing, Microsoft Teams, and video learning. When necessary, they can bring people in to do some training, but they do their onboarding remotely for the most part. New employees have software platforms to learn, especially those that keep track of billable hours. In addition, new employees have buddies that teach them all the various processes within the firm.

Remote working and onboarding have their challenges, but because of that, Paul feels that they've gotten pretty good at identifying the type of person that thrives in the environment that they offer. Their employees must be self-motivated since they can't rely on somebody to prod them along.

Paul also traces a lot of their success to gratitude being a foundational value within the group. They look for ways to constantly express appreciation, acknowledgment, and gratitude for everything that everybody does all the time. Their culture is awash in gratitude. The Rea Way sets the expectation that if they treat people right, they won't leave.

Because turnover is time-consuming and complicated from a client service perspective and a quality control perspective, Paul is grateful that they don't have very much turnover. People come, and they stay. They make a career at Rea, which is rare in today's environment. Paul feels that their focus on gratitude encompasses everything they do and makes a huge difference in their culture, especially with the great resignation in full steam.

Recognition and celebration are significant parts of their work environment. They are constantly looking for ways to acknowledge personal milestones and accomplishments. They also offer excellence bonuses to recognize people who go above and beyond. Not only do recipients of these awards get a nice thank you, but they also receive a monetary award. Rea remembers employee birthdays and work anniversaries with flowers and they look for any excuse to encourage people and let them know they appreciate everything they do. Paul feels it's working as he sees all of his people getting into it.

Once a week, during their team meetings, they allow team members to share what's going on personally – maybe there's something they're struggling with, or they want to share a personal win. These revelations have helped the Rea team build personal relationships and work well together. In addition, getting support when they need it and congratulations when they've accomplished something is a great way to acknowledge that their people are more than just employees.

Paul shared one of the interesting things that came out of this personal sharing time during their virtual meetings. It turns out that a spouse of one of their newer employees was also working at home at least part of the time. He was an engineer and had quite a few engineers that he supervised. His team did remote meetings, but they had focused only on business during their time together. After overhearing his wife's meeting banter, he incorporated more personal discussion into his sessions. He discovered that it made the meetings more fun and more productive as well.

Reflection points:

1. In how many ways do you acknowledge your people for a job well done? Make a list and see what you can add to it.
2. How can you add more personal connection and sharing time in your meetings?
3. Think about your hiring practices. Are you hiring people with the right attitude and training them on skill development, or do you look for industry experience first? How are your current hiring practices working out for you?

Remote Working: How to Connect with Employees, No Matter Where They Are

"Success in a hybrid work environment requires employers to move beyond viewing remote or hybrid environments as a temporary or short-term strategy and to treat it as an opportunity."
~George Penn, VP at Gartner

On March 1, 2020, I presented a keynote program in the Bahamas. A few people couldn't make it to the event because of some virus they called Covid. On March 3, I presented a different keynote in St. Petersburg, Florida. Again, a few people couldn't attend, but for the most part, the conference went on. It was business as usual. I didn't give Covid a second thought.

As a full-time professional speaker, I had a full calendar for the spring, summer, and into the fall. I didn't think that Covid would last past the end of April – or, in a worst-case scenario, mid-May. I looked forward to getting through another month or so when life would get back to normal. I had no idea how wrong I was.

A couple of weeks later, on March 15, 2020, the governor of Ohio shut down the state. We had our "stay at home" orders, and the world as we knew it came to a crashing halt. Essential workers, including manufacturing, grocery, and healthcare, continued to work, but all other "non-essential" companies had to figure out how to keep their businesses running.

Because my business was primarily working with clients at live events, I had to adjust to this new meeting environment. Virtual keynotes, training session, and conferences became my new reality. I even had the opportunity to present at a conference as an avatar – talk about a complete change in your business!

As the pandemic caused companies to alter their work practices, employees soon discovered they had many options regarding how, when, and where they could work. Soon, remote working became the rule instead of the exception. During the height of the Covid-19 pandemic, 62% of Americans worked from home, many for the first time in their careers. As time went on, Gallup data showed that 59% of remote workers preferred the flexibility of continuing working from home as much as possible after the pandemic. In comparison, 41% chose to return to the office. Over time, a third option gave employees the best of both worlds - the hybrid workplace.

All these work options have positives and negatives. However, no matter which you choose, you'll want to create a sense of cohesion that helps ALL employees thrive — no matter where and when they work.

Leaders must figure out how to balance engaging their on-site and remote employees. Providing purpose and direction so that all workers are on the same page creates a sense of unity. In addition, by evaluating each employee's role in decision-making and identifying ways to track and measure productivity levels, managers receive the wide-ranging input and feedback needed to ensure the job gets done.

If your employees successfully worked from home during the pandemic, you may want to reconsider your decision to bring them back to the office full time. Although you do have employees who like coming to work every day, giving them the option to work at home occasionally may offer them the flexibility they want while still allowing them to do their job efficiently.

Offering a hybrid workplace allows your team members to work in the manner that best suits them. For example, perhaps you let employees work from home two days a week and come into the office for three – or vice versa. As many organizations have discovered, employing a hybrid model makes for happier, more productive employees. It also reduces the resources used by the staff, including office supplies, utilities, and commute times.

Remote working is no longer a privilege granted only to a select few; many companies now build it into their job descriptions. As a result, the hybrid model gives employees the flexibility they want and expands the pool of potential employees and employers as a local staff is no longer a necessity.

Some benefits of a hybrid workplace include:

- **Flexibility**. Employees have the freedom to choose how and where they can best get their work done. They know where they are most productive, and they feel their bosses trust them because their managers empower them to make their own decisions.
- **Financial Gains**. Companies may cut back on office space and other overhead expenses. Not only will they make more money from increased productivity, but they'll also save the money they were spending on office supplies and utilities.

- **Productivity.** Employees get to focus on the work at hand instead of the constant interruptions they experience during a day in the office. Also, reducing an employee's commute time reduces stress, saves them money in gas and auto maintenance, and allows them more time to get their work done.
- **Talent pool access.** If your staff can do their job from anywhere, it doesn't matter where they live, giving you a bigger pool of candidates from which you can hire your industry's top talent.
- **Competitiveness in the marketplace.** As your company's job postings reflect flexible work options, you increase the attractiveness of your opportunity to applicants who have grown accustomed to a hybrid option.

If you're considering offering your employees the opportunity to work remotely full time, here are a few of the disadvantages you (and they) may want to consider.

- **Decreased collaboration.** Employees have more opportunities for impromptu exchanges, quick decision-making, and on-demand meetings when working onsite. Remote employees don't have the same opportunities to participate in hallway and watercooler conversations with their colleagues.
- **Fewer client interactions.** People like to do business with people they know, like, and trust. So, when clients don't have in-person access to their reps, it may negatively impact the relationship. However, using platforms like Zoom and Microsoft Teams can keep those personal interactions strong.
- **Less effective onboarding.** New employees won't have the opportunity to experience "a day in the life" with their coworkers. It

also makes it more difficult for them to ask questions and learn their jobs effectively, potentially slowing their career progression.
- **Decreased visibility**. Unless company leaders focus on results from both on-site and remote employees, they may favor the people they see regularly. Remote workers don't have the same chances to build personal relationships as their counterparts.

In all these scenarios, communication is essential. Although it may be easier to keep in touch with the people working on-site, remembering to over-communicate with your remote workers will keep them engaged and in the loop. Make sure to find out team members' preferred method of staying in touch - email, text, video conference, phone, app, etc. Ask how often they desire to hear from you. Conducting short pulse surveys every sixty days will help uncover any gaps in workplace satisfaction. When you encounter issues, do what you can to fix them immediately. Paying attention to your employees' needs and wants makes them more likely to trust you and stay with you for the longer term.

Holding your meetings over a video platform (Zoom, Teams, Google Meet) gives you the best of both worlds. You give everyone the chance to connect face-to-face, without having to get in a car or on a plane. The key to improving engagement during video meetings, though, is in encouraging your team members to turn on their cameras and making sure everyone has a chance to talk. You'll build trust and rapport with your staff, which will help them care more about you, their job, and the company.

There are challenges with a half-Zoom, half in-person meeting. When people gather in person, it's easier to read and respond to body language shifts. In a virtual environment, these skills are compromised. To determine the overall energy level of the group, you may want to take a minute and give each person a moment to reflect on how they feel about a group discussion on a scale of 1 (low passion/energy) to 10 (high passion/energy). Simply acknowledging that you care about their engagement level may lead to higher interaction and interest during your meetings.

Using video conferences also helps to assuage the feelings of isolation that tend to plague remote employees. When employees see a colleague's smiling face or pick up on minor nuances in body language while holding a conversation, they are more likely to feel connected, leading to a more robust company culture.

Just like the informal conversations you have with employees and colleagues in the workplace, during video calls, make sure you're paying attention to the personal side of employees' lives during your discussions. Regularly ask about how they're doing personally and notice any signs of what they are not saying. Then, see what you can do to support their situation and let them know you have their back.

Make sure you allow time to recognize the excellent work of your team members. Giving employees insight into their colleagues' accomplishments creates an opportunity for the identified person to feel celebrated while giving their peers the chance to add to the praise. Through regular social recognition, your team can continue celebrating each other's success every day, making everyone feel valued and appreciated.

To keep all employees – on-site and remote – on the same page, look for ways to keep your work resources, discussions, and activities in one central, digital place. In doing so, you'll give everyone access to everything they need to do their job. If you are ever considering an action that could leave remote team members in the dark, you may want to forego that option. Instead, ask for suggestions of how you can best serve both internal and remote team members.

Consider taking advantage of social media platforms to keep your workforce engaged and connected—host informal happy hours, games, or contests to connect socially and add fun to the mix. Encourage team members to share what's going on in the office and at home. Let people introduce their pets and children while online and find ways to let everyone see the personal sides of their colleagues.

Obtaining feedback can be difficult enough when people are working in the office. However, throwing in the challenge of the hybrid or remote workplace makes things even harder. To improve your chances of getting authentic feedback from your remote employees, you may want to incorporate technology. Using digital tools streamlines your feedback processes and makes it easy for remote employees to participate actively. Apps such as Slack and GroupMe keep everyone in the loop. Adding video conferencing, digital whiteboards, and shared drives involves all members of the team – no matter where they work. When employees feel heard, and managers act on their ideas and suggestions, they feel valued and are more likely to stay with you.

Another way to ensure that you're receiving authentic feedback from your "away" team is to be okay with anonymous answers. According to a Forbes report, 74% of workers would be more inclined to share feedback if they knew it would stay anonymous. Although managers may not like what this feedback uncovers, providing anonymous channels for feedback helps create a more engaged, psychologically safe workplace.

Whatever your employees share with you, you must embrace their feedback. By being proactive in your approach to getting employee feedback, your employees will feel safe to share their ideas, suggestions, worries, and concerns. They are also more likely to be engaged. When team members keep silent, it can cause a slow disengagement that leads to their quitting your company. Consider all feedback a gift. Address any issues openly and transparently and with the attitude of "thank you for sharing." Then, do something about it.

As department store founder, Marshall Field, once said of his customers, "Those who enter to buy, support me. Those who come to flatter, please me. Those who complain teach me how to please others so that more will come. Those only hurt me who are displeased but do not complain. They refuse me permission to correct my errors and thus improve my service." In considering your employees' feedback, remember that if they do not share their negative feedback with you, they refuse you the opportunity to make things right and keep them working for you and not your competition.

It can be challenging to treat remote and in-person workers as equals. However, training your managers to focus on outcomes rather than individual actions helps. Work to put as much thought and effort into planning online activities as you would in-person ones to encourage all employees to participate. Your company's core values determine your company culture. Train your managers to look for, acknowledge, and reinforce value-driven behavior on-site and in digital settings. When you take the time to recognize when team members are exemplifying core values, you ensure a more collaborative workplace.

Remote Working: Action ideas:

Individuals:

1. Determine which parts of your job you do best at home and which responsibilities you do better at work. Be open to working with your managers to determine the most effective scheduling.
2. Turn on your camera and participate in the discussion while online. Adding your personal touch to the meeting helps in the engagement levels of everyone involved.
3. Stop multitasking during meetings. When you give your full attention during the session, it increases the likelihood of having the information you need to be more productive.

Management:

1. Require that meeting participants be on camera unless they must tend to an emergency before rejoining. Be okay with a more casual appearance than you may expect for on-site meetings.
2. Incorporate fun activities and personal conversations during the meeting. Try to replicate the hallway and watercooler conversations your team members would be having if they were together in person.
3. Set your staff up for online success. If needed, spend time with individuals coaching them to set up their cameras, minimize background distractions, and effectively use the platform tools.
4. Ask employees if they prefer in-house, hybrid, or remote working. Then, set goals and create a plan for them to be successful.

Organization:

1. Assess which positions you need to have on-site and which employees can effectively work remotely or hybrid. Build flexibility into your job descriptions.
2. Schedule regular video meetings and provide opportunities for social interactions so that all employees can get to know each other personally and professionally. Make sure your leadership team is active and involved in these conversations.
3. Adopt the technology that makes it easy for your team members to communicate with each other and with you.
4. Ask for feedback and act on the ideas and suggestions received.
5. Focus on outcomes and results instead of the hours and days it takes to get the work done.

Use Your Website and Social Media to Showcase Your Company Culture

"We're living at a time when attention is the new currency. Those who insert themselves into as many channels as possible look set to capture the most value."
~Pete Cashmore, Founder of mashable.com

As part of the Americas Regional Management team at Baluff Americas, Will Healy, III loves providing strong customer stories, creating value for manufacturers, and coordinating Baluff's global strategy. As someone in the GenX/Millennial generation, Will grew up using technology. As a business professional, he knows the importance of having a great website and using social media to attract and retain your workforce.

Will feels that the best companies showcase their people and technology on their website and social media. One of his favorite examples is an automotive tier supplier. Every day this company shares posts and pictures featuring their people. In addition, they post photos and videos highlighting their technology, letting people know what a fun and fantastic place it is to work there. This extra effort strengthens their ability to recruit, hire, and retain their employees in a very competitive marketplace.

As for social media, Will prefers LinkedIn. He calls it digital Rolodex, so every time he receives a business card, he uses it as a reminder to find that person on LinkedIn. It's a powerful tool to connect with people individually. Will is not alone in his commitment to connecting on LinkedIn. Think about your social media presence. Are you posting exciting and attractive content to attract Millennial and Gen Z employees? If not, you may want to reconsider your social media practices.

With over 49% of the world's population using some form of social media - nearly 4 billion people – this is a part of your business you don't want to ignore. Your website plays a huge role in your market exposure.

When a potential employee visits your website, what do they see? Do they see people who look like them, or are there a bunch of stock images? By showing what an actual day in the life looks like in your facility using video interviews, photos, and facility tours, you have a higher likelihood of people wanting to check you out.

Your website is a digital door to your business. When a candidate goes to your site, it takes about 30 seconds to convince that applicant to join your team - or not. Your website needs to convey both your business brand and your employment brand. You can do this by clearly communicating your business's fundamental values and mission. When checking out your site, potential employees should get a sense of what it's like to work for your business.

Yes, you want to include basic information like location, number of employees, executive bios, and company history, but those facts don't necessarily showcase your company culture. Adding short videos, including virtual tours of the facility, interviews with employees about what it's like to work there, footage of social events, and recent community or service events, will set your company apart from most other businesses that that candidate is considering applying to.

Keep the application process simple. If your process seems complicated because of the number of steps or the amount of time it takes for you to respond, those potential employees will take their skills elsewhere. In addition, using an email autoresponder to let the applicant know that you received their paperwork along with a thank you note reinforces your company brand.

Your employer brand is how outsiders view your business. In a competitive talent marketplace, you must regularly monitor your company profile on LinkedIn and Glassdoor to see what current and past employees say about your company. If you're not familiar with Glassdoor, this is a site where satisfied and disgruntled current and former employees post their opinions about working for your organization. They tell it like it is. They write the good, the bad, and the very ugly. If the reviews are reasonable, it minimizes your risk when attracting candidates to apply for your positions. However, don't ignore bad reviews.

Taking a moment to address the issues that former or current dissatisfied employees are posting makes it evident that you care and are taking the time to respond. These review websites can also give you some insight into areas to focus on as you look for ways to upgrade your company culture. Some comments may be totally without merit, but then again, many may contain a seed that can lead to a more significant problem if not resolved.

Your brand must be authentic and consistent. Each piece of new content should advance your company's overall story. Your website, social media, and email list may be powerful tools for attracting new employees.

Here are some ideas to help you attract the right employees using your website, email, and social media.

1. **Create your employee avatar.** Narrow down the type of applicants you want to target. The easiest way to do this is to look at your current employees and find one you wish to duplicate. Then, write your job listing with that employee's traits and interests in mind, and you'll increase your chances of finding people who are like them.
2. **Know where potential employees hang out online.** Make sure you're placing job openings on the right social platforms. For example, if your potential employees aren't on Facebook, don't advertise there. Instead, figure out where they like to hang out and post your job listing on that site instead.
3. **Use employee advocates.** When your current employees promote your business on social media, it reflects how positive your working environment is. Share employees' posts on your company's social media and your website. Using video testimonials from staff is a great way to showcase the people and culture you have.
4. **Show what makes your company unique.** Because 64% of candidates research a company they're interested in online, you need to have relevant information available for that top talent to find. It's interesting to note that 37% of candidates will move on to another job opening if they can't find any information on the company they're applying for. Include photos of your facility - both inside and outside, particularly if you have lovely grounds. Show off the work area and any projects your team has participated in. Post any awards and recognition that you've received.

5. **Update your website.** If your website is outdated, old, and not up to modern standards, potential employees may not be interested in working with you. On the other hand, a professional-looking website shows that you care about your reputation. Also, make sure your website is mobile-ready.
6. **Regularly post on social media.** Almost everyone is on social media, and they often look for jobs using social media. It's true - 79% of job applicants use social media in their job search. Make sure you use the stories feature on social media.

Your website and social media presence are an applicant's first exposure to your organization in many cases. By paying attention to your online reputation and company brand, you increase the likelihood that your industry's top talent will find you – and not your competition.

Social Media and Website: Action Ideas:

Individuals:

1. Review your company's social media policy to make sure you comply with what you are posting.
2. Keep all posts respectful as they reflect your professionalism and credibility online.
3. Make sure all of your social media posts show your company in a positive light. If your mother would disapprove, don't post it!

Management:

1. Regularly communicate the do's and don'ts for social media posting.
2. Encourage employees to share positive posts about their experience working with your company.

3. Allow team members to share open positions on their social media pages to potentially encourage their friends and family to apply.
4. Take pictures at company events and outings and post them online (with employee permission) and display them in employee areas so they can relive the fun.

Organization:

1. Define your brand voice. Consider why your brand exists, what it values, how you describe it, and how you want customers to feel when interacting with your brand.
2. Measure the results to optimize your social media campaigns.
3. "Secret shop" your website. Check to see that the site shows the most up-to-date news and technology.
4. Go through your online application process. How easy is it to find the application? How simple is it to apply? How many ways do you offer for a candidate to apply to work for you?
5. Maintain a clear and detailed social media policy.

Volunteerism: Case Study: Teresa Lindsey, Channel Products

> *"You make a living by what you get. You make a life by what you give."*
> ~Winston Churchill

Because people have an innate desire to be a part of something bigger than themselves, giving employees opportunities to get involved with charitable causes during work hours goes a long way in creating camaraderie and increasing their commitment to the company. For Teresa Lindsey, CEO of Channel Products, philanthropy is an essential part of their culture.

Teresa allows her people to volunteer for causes they hold dear. Of course, employees must fill out a form and have it approved by management - after all, it's not a vacation day. But employees get paid for the day, making it a win/win. Sometimes groups of people or entire departments team up for more extensive, collaborative projects. The leaders of Channel Products constantly look for ways to create a unique experience for their staff, so, rather than writing a check to a charity, they get their people involved in the process.

When asked about her favorite volunteer group activity, Teresa shared how she surprised her staff with a fun day of giving back to their community. She divided her employees into four groups and took them out on limo-buses, challenging them to do as much charitable work in three hours as possible. Management gave each team matching t-shirts and $250 in cash. Their first goal was to put together a plan. They then told their drivers where they wanted to go and what they wanted to do, and the drivers followed their instructions.

To make sure the numbers were accurate, team members had to take a picture of everything they did and text it back to management. Managers then tallied up the points back at home base and awarded prizes in categories including who did the most random acts of kindness? Who does the coolest, most unique thing? Who brought back the most money? Who did genuine random acts of kindness without spending money?

In their three hours together, her team members accomplished over 100 random acts of kindness. For example, they brought coloring books and crayons to the children's unit at the hospital. They took supplies to the fire and police departments. They gave Gatorade to construction workers, paid for someone's gas, and even stopped at a drug store and paid for a person's prescription.

Teresa and the team at Channel discovered that there is more to volunteering than the "feel good" response that comes from giving back. Numerous studies show a positive correlation between employee engagement and company-sponsored volunteer programs. When employees work together in new ways, it provides unique experiences to learn about each other and build relationships outside of the workplace.

Here are a few studies that demonstrate the value of volunteerism in the workplace:

- VolunteerMatch: employees who volunteer through their workplace report more positive attitudes towards their employer and colleagues. They also have improved physical and emotional health. That means that if companies want to decrease their health costs, they should look to volunteering as an affordable and accessible solution.
- UnitedHealth Group Health: 64 percent of employees said that volunteering with work colleagues strengthened relationships.
- Cone Communications: 74% of employees feel more fulfilled at their job when they have opportunities to make a positive impact on social or environmental issues. The percentage for Millennials is even higher - at 88%.
- A study in Ireland: 87% of employees who volunteered with their companies reported an improved perception of their employer. More importantly, a whopping 82% felt more committed to the organization where they worked.
- PwC: "employees most committed to their organizations put in 57 percent more effort on the job and are 87 percent less likely to resign than employees who consider themselves disengaged."
- Gallup: "organizations that are the best in engaging their employees achieve earnings-per-share growth that is more than four times that of their competitors. Compared with business units in the bottom quartile, those in the top quartile of engagement realize substantially better customer engagement, higher productivity, better retention, fewer accidents, and 21% higher profitability. Engaged workers also report better health outcomes." So, where do employee volunteer and skills giving programs factor in? It's an excellent, relatively low-cost way to engage and retain employees.

Establishing an employee volunteer program has long-lasting benefits. But, before you jump in, it's essential to think about how the structure and scale the program. Some of the questions to ask before embarking on your volunteerism program:

- Will you offer paid time off to your employees to volunteer?
- Should you offer pro bono services or focus on hands-on volunteering?
- How will you allocate your volunteer time between public programs, visitor services, behind-the-scenes activities, fundraising events, and community outreach?
- What roles do you foresee volunteers playing?
- What fiscal resources are available to your volunteer program?
- Have you considered partnership opportunities with a nonprofit organization?
- How will you advertise your volunteer program to your employees?

Just like Teresa saw the benefits of volunteerism at Channel Products, here are three reasons you may want to consider giving your employees service opportunities outside of work:

Creates a sense of community. When you pair your company values with related charitable causes, you demonstrate that you genuinely care about a greater mission. Your employees notice - and so do your customers.

Builds relationships. You can use volunteer opportunities for positive team building. As your employees work together for a cause, they create strong relationships and social networks, making them less likely to quit.

Enhances skills. Working on projects outside of the office allows your team members to practice leadership, problem-solving, communication, interpersonal, and time-management skills.

Whether you take time off once a quarter or once a year to participate in a charitable project, why not give your employees the gift that keeps giving - their time and effort to serve a cause greater than themselves. You'll see the difference - both inside and outside of your workplace.

Volunteerism – Action Ideas:

Individuals:

1. Volunteer for the health benefits: a Carnegie Mellon study found that 200 hours of volunteering per year correlated to lower blood pressure among the volunteers.
2. Share your volunteer activities on your social media platforms. As you spread the word, you may encourage more people to get involved.
3. Volunteering may impact your future career. Your volunteer experience tells potential employers that you are ambitious, care about your community, and are willing to put in the effort that brings change.

Management:

1. Put together a program to offer opportunities for employees to get involved in charitable projects. Create parameters and expectations for all participants and follow up with them afterward.
2. Look for opportunities to get involved in volunteer opportunities as an organization or individual departments.
3. Promote your charitable activities on your website and online. You'll attract applicants who are looking for ways to make a difference.

Organization:

1. Build volunteer days into your business culture to build camaraderie between employees and foster relationships within the community.
2. Consider taking the pro-bono route and lend your services free of charge. For example, if your business has some extra space that's not being used at night or on weekends, consider contacting a nonprofit and offering it to them.
3. Sponsor charitable events in your community to weave a spirit of philanthropy into your company culture. You can make a financial contribution or raise money through raffles, silent auctions, etc.

Engagement Strategies to Elevate Employee Wellness and Mental Health

"We are embedding health and wellbeing at the heart of our business strategy because our people are our greatest asset, and we recognize that a healthy, happy, and committed workforce is vital to our business success."
~ Alex Gourlay, MD, Boots UK

Sometimes business leaders focus so much on the health of their company that they overlook the health of their employees and perhaps, even themselves. Because employees spend the bulk of their time at work, they often don't have the time to seek out wellness resources independently. Instead, many people rely on their employers to provide these opportunities. If your staff can't find these opportunities within your company, there's a good chance that they will look for them elsewhere.

The wellness industry is a $4.2 trillion market that continues to grow. Not only are employees interested in healthy habits and lifestyle choices, but they are also looking for employers who understand their need for better physical and mental health. By taking the time to research and invest in a wellness program, you're showing your employees that you care. When you pay attention to the health and wellbeing of your staff, not only is it good for them, but it is also excellent for your company's bottom line. Keep in mind that a one-size-fits-all approach to wellness does not work!

Steve Pacilio is the President of the Lift-All Company, Inc. A few years into his tenure, he noticed that many of his employees didn't have a primary care provider. Every time they got sick, they went to the emergency room for care. This habit was not only a bad option for the employees, but it was also expensive for the company. Steve found a lack of communication among management, Human Resources, and the employees about the benefits and the wellness options available.

Steve and his managers began to seek out employees who could act as their change agents. They scheduled meetings with these staff members to talk about wellness. As those people started to understand the need for a change in how they currently approached health, they shared their knowledge with other employees. Slowly and surely, the word spread around the plant. It took several years to implement the process, but they've developed what Steve calls an "unbelievable wellness program" where employees can earn up to $1400 in credits for the following year by going through biometric testing and seeing their doctor for an annual physical.

Today, most of their people have healthcare providers. So this program has been good for the company's financials and an excellent way to show their team members that taking preventative steps to keep themselves healthy is good for them.

Think about the healthy habits of your employees. Do you see a fit, energized group of people who take care of themselves physically and emotionally, or do you see an out-of-shape, lethargic group who is just trying to make it through the day before going home to their beer, pizza, and potato chips? Laura Timbrook, a Wellbeing Strategist and Speaker shares a story of what can happen when companies offer healthy alternatives, and their employees take advantage of them.

A client hired Laura to work with their employees to implement a new wellness initiative. Kate was among the people on the staff. Now, Kate liked Mountain Dew; okay, Kate LOVED Mountain Dew. Not only did she drink several cans a day, but she also had no interest in working out or making any changes to her slug-like habits at the end of the workday. Kate's employer brought in Laura to help the employees through the process, and leaders encouraged staff to get involved in these initiatives. But unfortunately, Kate was one of the most resistant to the change.

At first, Laura felt like she was beating her head against a brick wall with Kate. Every time she sat with her, she could feel Kate's resistance to her suggestions. But the interesting thing was, Kate kept coming back to talk to her. Perhaps it was because she thought that Laura wasn't judging her; Laura listened. Over time, Laura convinced Kate that it was safe for her to share her fears about how hard it would be to undo years of neglect. She encouraged Kate to give up one can of Mountain Dew each day and replace it with water. After a time, Kate switched two cans to water, and she kept going.

Fast forward two years - Kate got down to one Diet Mountain Dew per day. She drinks it because she enjoys it, not because she needs it. Kate is also kickboxing four days a week and has lost significant weight. As a result, she has more energy and vitality and feels better about herself than in years.

The great part of the story is that Kate was getting ready to retire right before she started participating in this wellness program. But, as she continued, she felt better and discovered she enjoyed her job more. The program made her feel like management cared about her and her wellbeing, so she decided to stay. Kate had been with the company a long time – thirty-plus years – and instead of losing all her skills, company knowledge, and expertise, her company retained a valuable, productive, and now healthier employee.

When organizations focus on an employee wellness program, they affect individuals – like Kate – but they also impact the entire organization over time. As far as the "rest of the story" with Kate, not only did she stay with the company, but she also recommended her Millennial daughter to come and join her. As demonstrated with Kate, as your workforce ages, investing in their health is one of the surest ways to retain your valuable employees. Millennial and Gen Z employees reported that they want wellness, family, and purpose as the top three attributes in their careers. Focusing on wellness initiatives also attracts new employees, like Kate's daughter, to join your organization.

Although many companies don't have the time, resources, or physical space to put a gym in their facility, they can still encourage their team members to get up and do something active. Research shows that when companies offer some exercise programs, and their employees are active for at least thirty minutes per day, company productivity increases by fifteen percent. So not only will you get more work done, but there's also a good chance your insurance premiums may go down.

There is a whole gamut of ways to increase employee wellness. Some ideas cost very little, while others come with an investment of tens of thousands of dollars in facilities and equipment. It doesn't matter where you start, as long as you begin with something. Be creative and ask your team members for their input.

One low-cost way to get started is to measure off routes and create a lunchtime walking goal for your employees. Put together a "mileage chart" to inspire employees to get involved. You may also want to provide pedometers or encourage your employees to download an app to keep track of their progress. Encourage standup or walking meetings – preferably outdoors so employees can also benefit from fresh air and sunshine. Finally, recognize when employees reach certain milestones and celebrate their successes, no matter how small they seem.

Exercise is one path to optimal health; diet is another. Companies that provide free lunches or healthy snacks are experiencing benefits that don't break the bank. According to one survey, sixty percent of employees feel more valued when they have a free lunch program. You can also provide healthy snack options instead of the usual junk food selections found in most vending machines. Many delivery companies bring in food and provide nutritional and background information about what the employees are eating. You may also consider a unique fruit or vegetable delivery program that introduces employees to and educates them about new foods they can try at home.

As a word of caution: before you create a program that you THINK will work for everyone, ask your employees for their ideas, suggestions, and recommendations. Because they are the people you want the buy-in from, asking employees to share their guidance will help increase overall participation rates. Again, there is no one-size-fits-all solution.

When you start your program, you may want to incentivize employees by offering prizes such as a Fitbit, smartwatch, PTO, gift cards, and more. Participation generally increases when there are reasons to do so. Over time, momentum will build, and employees will have the motivation they need to continue.

Wellness is more than physical health. It's about mental health as well. Ray Brown, President of the Esco Group, discovered that one in four employees went through some depression during the pandemic. Because of the potential long-term impact of this depression, they implemented an initiative called "Make it Okay." In this program, the wellness team created green t-shirts that said, "Make it okay to talk about mental illness."

Taking care of your workers and making sure that they are comfortable talking about uncomfortable topics like mental illness and depression creates a safe and accepting environment. From a mental health standpoint, people being cared for have a better chance of keeping themselves and everybody else working there safe.

It's essential to understand better the issues causing your team members workplace stress. Simply listening to them may alleviate some of the symptoms, as employees will appreciate that you are paying attention. Taking care of your employees' mental and physical health has bottom-line implications for your business. Every aspect of your workplace is impacted, including job performance, productivity, retention, and engagement.

Employees face a variety of challenges in their work-life and their home lives. When employers understand those challenges, it allows everyone to be their best selves. These programs also help create the best teammates, employee-owners, and partners for their manufacturing clients. Ray Brown says, "We are hopeful that every day we make our employees' lives a little bit simpler. Being our best and talking about mental illness is a big part of that mission."

It's up to you and the rest of your leadership team to reinforce the message. Use every communication channel possible to let your employees know what's available for their wellness needs. Besides encouraging THEM to get involved, make sure YOU set the self-care example.

One of the ways you can do this is to allow "healthy habit" time. After a long day, your employees may not be able or willing to devote time to health and fitness. Why not build some time into their day to allow them to participate in health-related activities like yoga, mindfulness, or strength training? When you create a culture that encourages self-care, your company and team will benefit from increased energy, motivation, and engagement.

Incorporating wellness initiatives is not only good for the heart and soul of your workforce, but with everyone's plates overflowing, these programs can play a significant role in reducing burnout. A Gallup study found that 23% of full-time employees feel burned out at work. This burnout accounts for $125 to $190 billion in health care spending due to increases in diabetes, heart disease, weight gain, high cholesterol, and mental health issues.

The problem is that burned-out employees are not only causing harm to themselves; they can also impact the productivity of their coworkers and the morale and culture of the entire company. Burnout can happen because of work overload. When you incorporate flexibility into employees' schedules and give them some say in how and when they get to do their work, it eases their stress level. Focus on results, not on the process of how the job is getting done.

Another way to reduce burnout as part of your wellness initiative may be to expand your flexible working policies. When employees know that they can take care of their children and elderly family members AND still get their work done, their stress decreases. The other good news is their commitment to your company increases. An added benefit is that by eliminating their commute, you'll save time and reduce the costs that impact your team and the planet.

When you create a culture that encourages self-care and pays attention to your employees' health and wellness, you will improve the health and prosperity of your business as well!

Employee Wellness: Action Ideas:

Individuals:

1. Be patient and consistent with your results. Your health challenges didn't happen overnight, nor will they change quickly.
2. Remember: You spend the first part of your life using your health to get wealth and the second part of your life using your wealth to get your health back. Choose self-care.
3. Thirty minutes of activity a day can be broken down into three ten-minute sessions. Look for simple ways to increase your movement throughout the day.

Management:

1. Create a safe space for employees to participate in programs and give them the time to do so.
2. Look for signs of burnout and adjust workloads and expectations accordingly.
3. Be approachable and make it okay to talk about mental health issues.
4. Find ways to get employees' family members involved to encourage better participation.

Organization:

1. Survey your employees to find out what benefits are most important to them. Compare that to the benefits you are currently offering and look for ways to upgrade your program.
2. Ensure that company leaders set the example for the rest of the team.
3. Focus on one health area each month: Diet, Fitness, Mental Health, etc., until it becomes ingrained in your culture.
4. Host a health fair to start the education process. Offer services like biometrics, so employees have a baseline for their health and can chart the progress they make.
5. Put together walking routes and encourage employees to get up and move during the day. Initiate standup or walking meetings to energize the participants.

The Role of Safety on Employee Engagement

*"You are your last line of defense in safety.
It all boils down to you".*
~ Kina Repp, a workplace accident survivor

July 22, 2006, was a beautiful early Saturday morning. Ray Brown, President of ESCO Group, and his mentor were on the golf course, getting ready to tee off. But unfortunately, Ray received one of those calls that, as a CEO President, you never want to get. He learned they lost a dear team member on that call to what could have been a very preventable electrical accident at one of their manufacturing facilities.

This super dedicated employee came into work early Saturday morning trying to get a project done so he could go and coach his son's baseball game. He did not make it to that game.

ESCO always prided itself on its excellent safety culture. However, six months before that 2006 incident, Ray was at a customer site, and one of their leaders was sharing the ESCO story with one of their customers. He joked with Ray, "You guys at ESCO are so serious. Don't take this the wrong way, but you're kind of like the safety Nazis."

And that customer was right. They always focused on safety. They made sure that everyone got trained correctly. They gave warnings for safety violations whenever they happened to keep their employees safe. They thought they had safety wholly covered. Then they had this event happen, and it's one of those things they never forget.

The life of the employee they lost is important, but it's also the lives of the family members that changed. Their employee had three kids and a wife who was battling cancer, who sadly passed away a short time after accident. Over time, ESCO learned from this failure so they could move forward. Even as tragic as this event was, they looked to make sense of the accident and use its lessons to enact positive changes for other folks.

ESCO took care of the employee's kids in the aftermath of the accident honoring their Dad's legacy and ensuring they were taken care of through college, including keeping in touch along the way. Thankfully, they grew up to be three very successful adults.

Another big piece of their safety journey is recognizing mental illness. ESCO called the program "getting awkward" so employees feel more comfortable having difficult conversations with each other. One of the initiatives they launched is "Make it Okay." They printed up green shirts that say, "Make it okay to talk about mental illness." Ray and his leadership team realize that everyone has different challenges that they're going through. Understanding those challenges, whether they're at home or work, allows people to be their best selves, as well as the best teammates, employee-owners, and partners for the manufacturers they support 27/7/365. When looking at how ESCO operates, Ray feels that they are simply an extension of the manufacturing process professionals out there.

Ray and Team introduced a unique way for his team members to "get awkward" after the safety incident. He had his employees write letters to their family members as if a horrific accident had happened. In those letters, employees shared everything they would want to say if they were no longer around to say it. Then, the recipients had to write a letter back to the employee letting them know why they would be missed. After that activity, Ray received many personal notes from spouses thanking them for taking the time to do that activity. Mental illness is a big part of keeping employees safe, and ESCO makes it okay to talk about those things.

When employees come to work, they rightfully expect to be safe. Providing a safe workplace is not only the right thing for companies to do, but it also has benefits for the organization. The Society of Human Resource Managers (SHRM) found that when employees are highly engaged, they have a five times lower risk of having a safety incident and a seven times lower chance of missing work due to safety mishaps.

A highly engaged employee is fully committed to doing their best work to contribute to their success. They put forth the more significant effort, go out of their way to ensure that they are doing things correctly, and actively offer their ideas, suggestions, and feedback.

Conversely, disengaged employees "check out" during safety meetings; they don't report minor injuries, near misses, or hazards in the workplace. In addition, they may take shortcuts, break the rules, and show a lack of respect for safety initiatives.

Management's behavior plays a crucial role in garnering trust, improving safety practices, and increasing worker engagement. Their skills and experience in dealing with their employees and safety procedures can help in fostering respectful relationships, building trust, opening two-way communication, and creating an empowering work climate. In addition, employee dealings with their managers and the safety staff often shape their perception of the organization's commitment to safety.

Part of the problem with disengaged employees may be unreasonable production goals where they have to choose between safety or cutting corners to complete their work. Ensure that you integrate your organizational and operational systems to avoid conflicting demands on the employee. In addition, listening to your team members and getting them involved in the process may foster engagement and positively affect safety.

The good news is when you focus on workplace safety, you increase engagement which leads to greater productivity, higher quality work, and higher retention rates. All this – and you're reducing the risk of a workplace accident or workers comp claims.

Use these tips to build a safer, more engaged workplace. However, do not force these actions upon your team. Instead, keep an open dialogue and invite your staff to offer feedback and opinions on the program processes. The more involved you allow your team members to become, the stronger the results and the better engagement level you'll get in return.

Keeping if Safe: Action Ideas:

Individuals:

1. Just like on an airplane, "if you see something, say something." First, watch out for unsafe behavior that can put your colleagues at risk. Then, report your findings to management and follow up to ensure they managed the problem.
2. If you are struggling, don't be too proud to get help. Many insurance plans have an EAP (Employee Assistance Program) that provides

confidential services and support for employees going through challenging times.
3. Look for ways to engage more in your job, your company, and with your colleagues. What do you love about doing what you do? By consciously focusing on the good, you will be more engaged and less likely to have a safety incident.

Management:

1. Remember that safety always applies to everyone. Just because you have a top producing manager or worker, you must take the steps necessary to correct their behavior if they are cutting corners and putting others at risk. You never know which of your other employees is watching that person's bad behavior, leading to a tragic outcome.
2. Provide ongoing education. Safety is not a "one and done" process. Hold regular briefings to keep the conversation going and their skills sharp. Provide the tools necessary for employees to do their job safely and make sure employees know how to use them. Make sure your safety procedures are concise, defined, straightforward, and easy to understand. Do not allow for grey areas.
3. Create a sense of respect and pride. Treat your employees as equals and let them know you respect them and the excellent work they do. People are more willing to listen and pay attention if they feel their employer cares about them. You also want to recognize your employees' efforts in keeping themselves and their coworkers safe. Put together a reward system that encourages good behavior. When employees take pride in their work and value their teammates, they will look out for each other and do their best to keep each other safe.

Organization:

1. Set Clear Guidelines. Emphasize your organization's commitment to safety and why it matters to you personally. Let employees know that you care about them and want to ensure they go home safely each day. Create standardized checklists to make it easier for employees to track what they need to do to stay in compliance with safety standards.
2. Encourage feedback. When employees are involved in the safety planning process, they are more likely to buy into it. Although safety is serious business, humor or gamification increases engagement levels. As employees go through the process, continuously ask for their feedback and then act on their suggestions. Get everyone involved and on board with your strategies. Remember that implementation takes time, so when minor mistakes happen, treat them as learning experiences instead of punishing them too quickly.
3. Involve employees. Encourage employees to share their opinions, concerns, and ideas and openly discuss any changes before implementing them. Keep your door always open and when you act on an employee's suggestion, give credit where credit is due. Not every idea that an employee shares will be good or constructive. Listen to them, show them respect, and be willing to consider additional options.

Additional Resources: Nontraditional Places to Find Employees

Nontraditional places to find employees

There is no easy or magic button to find good people in a tight labor market. However, by being creative and using your imagination, you can set yourself apart from other organizations fighting over the same people you are looking to hire.

Here are some ideas to help:

Veterans. With more than 200,000 U.S. service members returning to civilian life each year, this is an excellent resource for talent. Service members already have sought-after leadership qualities such as meeting deadlines, solving problems, supervising teams and working in extreme conditions. In addition, veterans have a strong work ethic, are team players who have received extensive training, are organized, dependable, and ready to work.

However, hiring a military veteran isn't just a noble thing for an organization. It's also a way to receive a tax break or tax credit. The Internal Revenue Service created the Work Opportunity Tax Credit (WOTC) program in the mid-1990s to encourage organizations to hire groups that traditionally had difficulty finding jobs. That list included ex-felons, welfare recipients, veterans, and victims of Hurricane Katrina.

Hiring veterans is also a way to show that your company understands and values veterans' contributions to the workplace. Because the military is one of the most trusted institutions in the United States, hiring veterans brings that trust and good reputation to the companies they work for. Ultimately, when companies hire veterans, it is a win/win/win – for the veteran employees, employers, and coworkers. Veterans have what it takes to be an asset to any organization they join.

Ex-Felons. When you are open to hiring people with previous convictions, you can significantly expand your applicant pool. Ex-offenders are often an incredibly hardworking group, which means higher productivity levels for you. Also, because many employers are unwilling to hire former felons, this group brings more loyalty and less turnover. They recognize that their opportunities are not as plentiful as those for other groups. These potential employees may have also taken training programs in prison, bringing developed and specialized skills to the workplace.

In addition to expanding your talent pool, your company may also benefit from government tax credits, wage reimbursement, or training funds by hiring ex-offenders. When you hire an ex-offender who works a minimum of 120 hours, you can claim a partial tax credit. If the person works 400 hours or more, you may claim the full tax credit. The maximum tax credit for ex-offenders per eligible individual is $2400. However, there are no limits to the number of individuals an employer may hire within these target groups. So, the tax credits could add up to significantly reduce an employer's tax burden.

Companies including Dave's Killer Bread, Quality Ingredients, Home Depot, American Airlines, and Under Armour have hiring practices inclusive of those with criminal records. As a result, job opportunities provide a second chance for ex-offenders to enter the workforce, start earning an income, develop valuable skills, and reduce the risk of going back to prison.

LinkedIn. One of my friends who owns a plumbing company found it almost impossible to hire master plumbers. Even with a $10,000 signing bonus, her coffers were coming up empty. So, she went on LinkedIn and found people who matched the description of whom she was looking to hire. She reached out to them with a direct, personalized video and received several responses. She was then able to hire directly from those videos.

Here are a few more ideas to use on LinkedIn:

- *Focus on your followers.* According to LinkedIn research, 58% of the people who follow your Company Page on LinkedIn want to work for you. People who follow you are also 95% more likely to accept an InMail message from you and 81% more likely to respond.
- *Clone your current top performers.* Look at the LinkedIn profiles of the people you have working for you. See how their backgrounds, experiences, and skills are like those you promote.
- *Make your personalized message short and sweet.* In other words, be bold, be brief, be gone. InMail messages under 100 words get the highest response rate. Also, be polite and conversational, and don't forget to thank the applicants for their time.
- *Be clear and concise.* Avoid acronyms, abbreviations, industry jargon, and company-specific names and phrases when drafting your job description. Don't try to be too fancy – use clear titles such as sales rep, software engineer, or project manager. Add salary,

qualifications, job details to help make sure you get your job in front of the right individual. Your job applications and descriptions must be transparent, accessible, and easy to follow. If you need some help, you can hire a writer to help your descriptions stand out and draw in more talent.

Always be looking: Whenever you receive excellent customer service at a restaurant, store, or other place of business, connect with that employee to find out how they feel about their job. You never know; you may be meeting them at a time when they are thinking about leaving. Another place to look is your customer list. Your customers are already your fans, so if you find someone who is excellent, why not see if they're keeping their options open.

Social Media. Your potential employees are probably checking you out online before they ever fill out an application. Make sure you post engaging content on all the different platforms - Facebook, Twitter, Instagram, and YouTube. You can also encourage your employees to post their favorable experiences with your company and let their friends know about open positions.

Email and Newsletters. If you're sending out any regular communications to your customers and prospects, such as emails or newsletters, make sure to mention that you're looking for great people to join your organization.

Employee Referral Program. Allow your employees and coworkers to recommend people they know for open positions. Give a reward when the new person starts and then six months and a year later to encourage retention.

Promote from within. You may already have the person you need working for you, but they're in a different position. Promoting from within cuts down on training and acclimation time, and it also shows employees and applicants that you offer growth opportunities.

Company Website. Because many job-seekers go directly to a company website to apply for a job, make sure your website is user-friendly, and pages for open positions and applications are easily accessible. If you haven't gone through your application process personally, try it to see how easy (or difficult) it is. If necessary, streamline your approach to get the essential information you need. You can then follow up with the most qualified candidates.

Colleges and Universities: Team up with your local community colleges, universities, and tech schools to connect with students ready to find jobs. By connecting with guidance counselors, professors, or the workforce development department, you have opportunities to bring in the new generation of talent.

Check your files: Sometimes, candidates slip through the cracks when you hire someone else for the position. If you keep that applicant's information on file, you can contact them when another job opens up.

Loosen Your Restrictions. Assess whether your open positions need a specific level of experience - or can you train them? Is a degree essential for this job? If not, adjust as necessary to attract more applicants.

Search Firms: Sometimes, you just need a little more help. By working with recruitment firms specializing in finding your specific talent, you'll speed up the process.

About the Author

Lisa Ryan, CSP, is the Chief Appreciation Strategist at Grategy. Her Grategy® programs focus on employee productivity and retention, gratitude strategies to boost your business and lift your life, generational issues, customer loyalty, and overall growth.

As a Certified Speaking Professional, Lisa helps organizations keep their top talent and best customers from becoming someone else's through her engaging, interactive, and fun keynotes, workshops, video series, and consulting assignments. In addition, Lisa is the author of eleven books and co-stars in two films, including the award-winning "The Keeper of the Keys" and "The Gratitude Experiment."

Lisa is a proud Cleveland, Ohio native. She received her bachelor's degree and MBA from Cleveland State University on the "fourteen-year" plan. She and her husband, Scott, have been married since 1996, and they are the proud parents of two very spoiled cats.

Relevant Experience

- Keynote, breakout, or workshop speaker at more than 1000 conferences and events
- Thirteen years of industrial marketing and sales experience, including seven years in the welding industry – **and yes, she does weld**

- Host of "Elevate Your Engagement Levels: What You Need to Know" on the Elite Expert Network
- Creator of "The Seven Mistakes Managers Make to Crush Company Culture" video series.

Bring Lisa to your next event:
www.LisaRyanSpeaks,
lisa@grategy.com
216-359-1134.
Copyright© 2022 Grategy, LLC and Lisa Ryan. All rights reserved. You may copy and share this information with proper attribution to the author.

To Order Additional Copies of This Book:

Share copies of THANK YOU VERY MUCH with participants at your next conference, workshop, retreat, or training program where you need ideas and strategies to jumpstart your engagement initiative.

Here is the quantity pricing for the direct purchase of the book. All discounts are savings from the retail price of $19.95.

25-100	$15.00 each
101-250	$14.00 each
250-499	$12.00 each
500 +	$10.00 each

Prices do not include shipping and handling.

Call for a complete pricing proposal or an estimate to your location.

Call or email: (216) 359-1134 or lisa@grategy.com

Visit our website for all the latest news:

www.LisaRyanSpeaks.com

Bibliography:

20 Unique Places to Find Qualified Employees - Successful Blog. https://www.successful-blog.com/1/20-unique-places-find-qualified-employees/

Could the Solution to The Great Resignation Be as Simple as Gratitude? A New Study Suggests Yes | Inc. Magzeine. https://www.inc.com/jessica-stillman/great-resignation-employee-retention-gratitude.html

Employee Recognition Programs | Guide for 2021 | O.C. Tanner.

https://www.octanner.com/insights/articles/2019/4/3/your_comprehensive_g.html

Ex-Offender Second Chances Could Mean Big Benefits for Employers. https://www.efficienthire.com/second-chances-could-mean-big-benefits-for-employers/

How to recognize and celebrate success at work | Impraise. https://www.impraise.com/blog/how-to-recognize-and-celebrate-success-at-work

Improving Safety Through Employee Engagement. CA Short. https://www.cashort.com/blog/employee-engagement-is-key-to-improving-workplace-safety-0

Managers are on Front Lines of Employee Safety Struggle .... https://www.hrexchangenetwork.com/employee-engagement/articles/managers-are-on-front-lines-of-employee-safety-struggle

Reasons To Hire Veterans. By MilitaryBenefits. https://militarybenefits.info/reasons-hire-veterans/

Remote Work Persisting and Trending Permanent. Lydia Saad, Ben Wigert, PhD. https://news.gallup.com/poll/355907/remote-work-persisting-trending-permanent.aspx

Ultimate Guide to Employee Onboarding - SaplingHR. https://www.saplinghr.com/employee-onboarding

Using LinkedIn Recruiter: 7 Tips to Help You Get the Most Out of It. Bruce M. Anderson. https://www.linkedin.com/business/talent/blog/product-tips/using-linkedin-recruiter-tips

Made in the USA
Monee, IL
03 June 2025